Presenting Performances

Thomas Wolf
Illustrated by Barbara Carter

Presenting Performances

Published in cooperation with the Association of Performing Arts Presenters

ACA Books
A Program of the American Council for the Arts
New York, New York
Copublished with Allworth Press

Published by American Council for the Arts
1285 Avenue of the Americas, 3rd Floor, New York, NY 10019

93 92 91 5 4 3 2 1

Book and Cover Design by Celine Brandes, *Photo Plus Art*
Typesetting by *The Desktop Shop*
Printing by *Capital City Press, Inc.*

Director of Publishing: Robert Porter
Assistant Director of Publishing: Doug Rose
Publishing Assistant: Tiffany Chez Robinson

Library of Congress Cataloging-in-Publication Data:

Wolf, Thomas, 1945–
Presenting performances / by Thomas Wolf : illustrated by Barbara Carter. — 6th ed.
p. cm.
"Copublished with the Association of Performing Arts Presenters".
Includes bibliographical references.
ISBN: 0-915400-98-7
1. Performing arts sponsorship—Handbooks, manuals, etc.
I. Title.
PN1590.S7W6 1991
790.2'068'8—dc20

91-32210
CIP

Contents

Preface

The first edition of this book appeared in 1977. At that time, many organizations presented performances, but only a small percentage had large budgets or professional staffs. Most presenting organizations were small, community-based enterprises staffed largely by volunteers. A decade and a half later, the landscape has changed. All-volunteer organizations still exist, but many small presenting organizations have matured and prospered—and have become fully professionalized. Even all-volunteer organizations have become far more sophisticated about the work they do.

This maturation of the presenting field in the last fifteen years is one of the reasons for the first substantial rewrite of *Presenting Performances* since its original publication. Not only were some of the precepts in the original volume out of date, but much of the advice did not go into enough depth. This new version supplements the most important basic information with tips that will be of use to first-time presenters and seasoned professionals as well.

The need for revised and expanded information was certainly one impetus for this new version of *Presenting Performances,* but it was not the only reason for revisiting the material with a fresh eye. At the time I had the original idea for the book, in the mid-1970s, there was great optimism about the performing arts presenting field. For the most part, that optimism was well founded. With rapidly increasing federal and state budgets for the arts, with a commitment

I encourage you to read this book on two levels. Read it first for its point of view about presenting as a nonprofit service. Then keep it, read it, and refer to it for the extensive technical advice it provides on managing a presenting organization. The field owes a debt of gratitude to the board of the New England Foundation for the Arts for first recognizing the importance of this publication to what was then a young field. In the fifteen years since it was first written, *Presenting Performances* has been a major resource. The Association of Performing Arts Presenters is proud to have this opportunity to work with Tom Wolf and the American Council for the Arts in carrying on this tradition.

Although this edition is updated, much has remained the same. Just as we have retained all of Tom Wolf's practical advice and insight, we have also kept Barbara Carter's wonderful illustrations and even added a few new ones. Once again the combination is both informative and entertaining. Read on and enjoy.

Susie Farr, Executive Director
Association of Performing
Arts Presenters

Introduction

This is the sixth edition of *Presenting Performances.* In the preface to the fifth edition, directors of state arts agencies in New England wrote: "A book like this is never finished. It needs updating and revisions as new fashions of presentations emerge and new management methods are discovered." This latest version of the book demonstrates the accuracy of their statement.

In the eight years since *Presenting Performances* was last revised, the growth in performing arts presenting has been dramatic. The field has become more professional, especially in its service to artists and communities. Organizations that began as good ideas in the minds of a few committed volunteers have become integral to the lives of their communities throughout the country. With such examples before them, new presenting organizations continue to spring up.

This growth has led to a greater understanding of presenting. We now can see it as a distinct and important field as well as an active and valuable activity for the arts. Presenting organizations have become more mission-driven and have learned to work more effectively in partnership with artists and communities. In many instances, presenters have also made substantial contributions to the development of art works and art forms. Although much of the standard administrative work of a presenting organization remains the same as it was when *Presenting Performances* was first published, the vision of presenting as a multifaceted function has grown considerably.

to cultural development throughout the United States, and with seemingly limitless potential for audience growth, the number of presenting organizations and presenter service organizations grew at an extraordinary rate. The original *Presenting Performances* was intended to provide necessary information to all these new presenters who were entering a world of incredible potential.

Today, presenters face the future with a greater sense of uneasiness. Audience growth has waned. There is more competition for people's recreational time, and it is increasingly difficult to lure many out of their homes and away from their televisions and VCRs. Costs for presenting the performing arts have escalated while revenue has not kept pace. Indeed, the budgets of the very federal and state agencies that fueled so much growth in the 1970s and 1980s are under attack and in many cases in jeopardy. Finally, there is another problem—societal needs in the last decade of the twentieth century have become so overwhelming in most parts of the United States that presenters are often being asked to do their part in addressing them. This has meant, at the very least, taking a hard look at organizational mission and programming philosophy as well as expanding outreach and education efforts.

These changes do not portend the grim outlook for the presenting field that many are now predicting. They do suggest an era of change in which old formulas may simply no longer work. This is another reason why it has been so important to update *Presenting Performances.* Although much of this book is similar to the earlier version, there are important changes in emphasis that reflect a different time—one in which there are still opportunities, but ones that look very different from what they once were.

Updating old material can be a less-than-exciting task. In this case, the task was stimulating and enjoyable because of my collaboration with Susie Farr, executive director of the Association of Performing Arts Presenters, the co-publisher of this book. Susie Farr read every word of the old draft, made line-by-line suggestions, and brought her superb insights to bear on the revisions. My thanks to her and to illustrator Barbara Carter, who deserves so much credit for the continuing popularity of *Presenting Performances.* I would also like to thank Robert Porter and the staff of the American Council for the Arts for their help in undertaking this new version of the book.

Thomas Wolf
Spring 1991

Get Organized!

1

Administration

Once upon a time there was a young man who decided that he would devote his life to the arts. The only question was, which one? He set out for the local music conservatory and presented himself to a piano teacher. "To play piano," he was told, "you will have to practice scales two hours a day for the rest of your life." Surprised and a bit disappointed, the young man walked across the street to the art institute and told his story to the painting instructor. "To become a painter," he was told, "you will have to learn first to draw simple shapes; later, we will let you paint still lifes of fruit and flowers." The local academy of drama was next. Our hero wanted *Hamlet;* the teacher suggested six months of calisthenics. Finally, in desperation, the young man paid a call on the local presenting organization. No sooner had he walked into the office and presented his case than he was seated at a word processor and told to produce a press release for the next week's event. ("Suddenly I was learning how to write excellent fiction," he later recalled.) As soon as he finished the press release, he was dispatched to the florist and told to select the display of flowers for the auditorium stage. ("What better way to show off my artistic eye!") Finally, when he returned to the office, he was given a list of phone numbers and told to do some telemarketing to sell tickets. ("Instantly I learned the rudiments of persuasive play acting.") By the end of the day, the young man had made up his mind. The most creative life in the arts for him was not in music, painting, or theater; it was in presenting the performing arts.

The story is, of course, apocryphal, but it is included here to introduce the idea that presenting the performing arts can be an extremely satisfying and creative occupation, whether you are a volunteer worker, a board member, or a paid administrator. Lest the story mislead, however, we must quickly point out that, contrary to the young man's notions, creative presenters are probably not the ones who simply choose floral arrangements and write press releases. Rather they are the ones who undertake long-range planning, set artistic goals in relation to community needs, establish realistic objectives, and achieve success through imagination and efficient management.[1]

RULE 1

Get ORGANIZED!

One presenter put it this way:

> Everything must begin with sensible planning. In our case, it did not. By just letting things happen we learned our lessons the hard way. For example, we learned that it is essential to think about fund raising before you need money. Today, we find ourselves back on track. We think one or two seasons ahead. We project budgets; we set artistic and administrative goals. For me, personally, the most exciting part is getting organized and translating those goals into reality.

In the course of this chapter, we will consider some of the critical issues in presenting the performing arts. It will become clear that presenting organizations need far more than gifted performers. They need people with business acumen, a promotional bent, some knowledge of the law, and a talent for efficiency and good organization. We will also see that the effective presenter is one who has developed an artistic philosophy that takes into consideration the need to entertain, educate, and touch people's lives in a variety of special ways.

RULE 2

Incorporate and protect your TAX-EXEMPT STATUS.

"Why a corporation?" many new presenters ask. "We are simply a handful of people—all volunteers—handling a tiny budget. Isn't the idea of forming a corporation a bit out of scale with the scope of our activities?" The answer to this question is probably no. A corporate structure allows your organization to apply for tax-exempt status, to enter into contracts with performers, to limit personal liability, and to secure credit. Without a corporate structure, carrying out the daily chores of the office soon becomes complicated: potential contributors turn their backs on you, stores refuse to open charge accounts, and individuals must be found who will take personal responsibility for signing contracts.

By far the most important advantage of a corporate structure is that it allows your organization to apply for and secure tax-exempt status—a process that generally takes about six months. Once tax-exempt status has been granted, individuals or businesses can contribute to the organization and deduct the donations for income-tax purposes. As a general rule, almost no one contributes to organizations that are not tax-exempt—it is simply too expensive to do so. Therefore, unless you can do without fund raising, you must either incorporate or become associated with an organization that is itself tax-exempt.

Why does the federal government grant tax-exempt status? Essentially, the idea is to encourage private organizations to carry out important service-related work that is less likely to get done well, if at all, by for-profit corporations or the government itself. Tax-exempt status is much like a public subsidy. The tax exemptions that donors claim on their tax returns is money not paid over to the Treasury. The government may give up potential tax revenues from the organization as well. For example, end-of-year surpluses are not taxed as profits but may simply be carried forward for future use in their entirety. Because the government is providing these various kinds of financial assistance, it is important for those connected with the nonprofit organization to make sure it is truly set up to carry out a public purpose. Thinking about the mission of the organization and its service to society is a prerequisite to securing tax-exempt status and should be a continuing concern once tax-exempt status is obtained.

For those who do not want to go to the time, expense, and trouble of incorporating and filing for tax-exempt status, a common solution is an arrangement by which a small presenting organization becomes

TAX EXEMPT
Incorporate and protect your TAX EXEMPT STATUS.

a "project" of a larger tax-exempt institution. Through such an arrangement, the presenting group might associate itself with a local arts agency, church, college, or community service organization. In doing so, however, the presenting organization risks losing some autonomy, and it can be subject to the whims of the parent organization's board of trustees. Sometimes the arrangement is successful and lasts indefinitely, but often trouble begins to brew when the growing presenting organization begins to expand its programming. A nervous board of trustees starts to feel uneasy about a large budget that is not under its close scrutiny. Many groups that begin as a project of a larger organization eventually find that separate incorporation is desirable.

However, this umbrella arrangement is an excellent temporary solution to the problem of securing tax-exempt contributions for new enterprises. Let us say that a group of people wants to set up a presenting organization, and each agrees to contribute $200 to the new venture. Because the organization is not tax-exempt, the contributions are not tax-deductible. If, however, during the first few months, the new organization can be listed as a project of the YMCA (or some other tax-exempt entity), then a separate account can be set up and checks can be drawn to "YMCA—Arts Account." In this way, contributions can be solicited from the first day of the new project with the understanding that they are tax-deductible.

For an individual without legal training, the procedures connected with incorporating and obtaining tax-exempt status are complicated and mysterious. For lawyers, however, these same procedures are fairly routine; moreover, it is not uncommon for lawyers to donate their services for incorporating a nonprofit organization. Often a lawyer will be invited to serve on the board of trustees after the corporation is formed. If a public-spirited lawyer cannot be found in your community, call your state or local arts agency to find out whether there is a chapter of Volunteer Lawyers for the Arts in your area. This agency may run a referral service on free or low-cost legal assistance for arts-related activities. Another possibility is to call your county or state bar association and ask for a referral.

Your lawyer will be busy during the first year of your new corporation. (After the first year, you will probably need legal assistance only occasionally.) The first thing the lawyer will do is write up your articles of incorporation and file these, together with the necessary forms, at the appropriate state offices. The cost of filing is modest. Once your organization has been granted corporate status, a set of bylaws must be written and approved (these generally follow a standard format for nonprofit corporations, and a sample version is contained in appendix A). As your lawyer will no doubt tell you, the Internal Revenue Service

(IRS) will review your articles of incorporation and bylaws carefully to determine whether you qualify as a tax-exempt corporation.

The bylaws should be flexible, and the board should feel free to amend them whenever necessary. As one lawyer put it, "In the bylaws, almost nothing is forever." From the very beginning, however, try to set things up so that corporate decisions can be made quickly and easily. Moreover, your lawyer may suggest a number of items that you feel are unnecessary, but unless they appear to run counter to your plans, let them remain in the document. There is a formula for writing bylaws, and the IRS does not like to see certain familiar paragraphs deleted.

After the bylaws are written, your lawyer will file an application for tax-exempt status. If everything goes smoothly, you can expect to receive a federal tax-exemption letter within several months. If there are any problems with your application, the IRS will send a letter to your organization suggesting certain revisions in the bylaws or the articles of incorporation. The federal tax determination is the critical document which will establish whether gifts to your organization are tax-deductible on federal and state tax returns and determine your exemption from most taxes. However, in some areas, you may require an additional state exemption certificate to provide vendors with evidence that you are exempt from state sales tax. Once the federal exemption is obtained, getting the state exemption form is generally a simple matter.

Once you have received tax-exempt status, the difficult part is over. However, it is a mistake to cease thinking about the corporate obligations of the board of trustees. The trustees must meet at certain times; minutes must be kept when meetings are held; and financial records must be filed with various state and federal agencies. All the records of the corporation (articles of incorporation, bylaws, tax-exemption letter, minutes, financial statements, and so forth) should be kept together, because they are open to scrutiny by state and federal authorities at any time. A common procedure is to put all records in a three-hole, loose-leaf binder which can be left with the secretary (sometimes called the clerk) of the corporation, with your attorney, or at the organization's office. Of particular importance is the actual "tax determination" letter in which the IRS officially grants tax-exempt status. In many fund-raising proposals, it will be necessary to submit a copy of this letter, so it should be kept in a safe place.

It is also well to remember that tax-exempt status can be revoked at any time if the IRS determines that an organization is not meeting the public purpose for which it was established. It is important for tax-exempt presenting organizations to distinguish themselves from commercial presenters through the kinds of educational and public service programs that they conduct. Trustees must remember that in a nonprofit presenting organization there is more to good practice than bottom-line considerations. In addition, at least every five years, such an organization should review its mission statement (contained in the articles of incorporation) and the bylaws, engage in a long-range planning process, and update these documents if necessary according to the directions of the planning effort.

It is also important to remember that potential contributors, government agencies, and business concerns tend to view a legally constituted nonprofit corporation as different from even the most respected and distinguished group of people who are loosely banded together. Armed with a Federal Employer's Identification number (which is like a social security number for corporations) and a tax-exemption letter, your legal and organizational status will be clear to everyone and your dealings with the outside world will be appreciably less complicated.

RULE 3

Pick your trustees with UTMOST CARE.

Some years ago, the executive director of a state arts council said the following in a speech to arts administrators:

> It seems remarkable to me that many of our arts organizations which maintain such high aesthetic standards are incredibly casual about their choice of trustees. How is it, I often ask myself, that an organization which subjects all of its performers to the most rigorous scrutiny can be so unconcerned about the selection of people who will, after all, have ultimate responsibility and be legally liable for the corporation's operation? Bad performers can be fired. But try to get rid of a bad board member and you will see how difficult it is.

The speaker then went on to give sound advice on the selection of good trustees.

First, think of every member of the board of trustees as someone with a specific job or responsibility. Do not invite anyone to serve simply because you think his or her name is important to your organization's credibility. Window dressing—that is, the use of distinguished names as an endorsement—can be achieved by forming a special committee of honorary advisers. Mayors, senators, famous performers, wealthy individuals, and others may be asked to lend their names to your endeavor by serving on an advisory committee, which

Pick your Trustees
with UTMOST CARE.

may never meet and whose services may rarely be required. However, the names of advisory committee members can be added to your letterhead. In this way they can show their support of your organization. You need not invite them to serve on the board of trustees.

Second, the board of trustees should be representative of the community as a whole. It must be culturally and racially diverse; it should include men and women, young and old; and it must incorporate a broad cross-section of an organization's potential constituents. Many presenters wonder why large segments of the community do not participate in or attend their programs. In many cases, it is because their boards of trustees are perceived to be elitist and exclusionary. Funders, too, are increasingly dismayed when the governing group of a presenting organization does not include many different kinds of people from the area it claims to serve.

Third, in searching out board members, begin by deciding what jobs and responsibilities need to be covered. Does the board need someone with expertise in law or business? Could a certified public accountant (CPA) be found who would be willing to assist in setting up the books? Is a well-to-do contributor needed who can be counted on for at least $2,500 each year? Perhaps there is a particular job, such as head of the marketing committee, that needs to be filled. Any of these are good reasons to appoint specific people with proper qualifications to the board. Match the organization's needs to particular people with particular skills. Do not begin by saying, "Mrs. J. would be so pleased to be on the board; she simply loves the concerts." Instead, think of the jobs that need to be done and find the best people to do them.

Fourth, do not hedge when you invite someone to serve on the board. Tell the person why he or she is being asked. Be direct about the responsibilities that are to be assumed. If a business executive is being put on the board in order to attract more funds from the business community, this fact should be clearly stated: "The board would like to increase business contributions by $20,000 over the next three years, and we would like you to be responsible for organizing the effort." If prospective board members turn you down, consider yourself lucky. You have been spared the frustration of putting up with people who would not be doing their share of the work.

Finally, every trustee should have a fixed term of office, which should not exceed three years. If, at the end of the term, the board member has performed well, he or she can be reelected to another term. But reappointment should not be automatic, and members of the corporation who vote on such matters should evaluate the trustee's performance carefully before reelecting. Today, most organizations limit the number of consecutive years a trustee can serve to five or six. Committed individuals will often continue volunteering or serving on committees after their board service is complete and, after a year or two, it may be appropriate to bring back the strongest of them to the board.

One of the most persistent problems facing small presenting organizations is that their boards of trustees do not take proper initiative in fund raising. In many cases, board members fail even to realize that if they approve a deficit budget they must help devise a sensible plan for raising the necessary funds. Many believe that the responsibility for raising funds rests with the staff. Some trustees buy tickets or give ten dollars each year and believe that their obligations in this area have been met.

Virtually any presenting organization should have a policy that each trustee contributes some cash above and beyond the price of a ticket each year. The amount of the gift may vary depending on the organization and the particular mix of trustees. Such a contributions policy demonstrates a level of commitment on the part of the board that may be important to other fund-raising prospects, particularly institutional donors. In addition, the board of trustees must take an active role in fund-raising activities, with each trustee either raising money personally or assuming some other task in the fund-raising effort, such as working on an event, writing "thank-you" notes, and researching corporate and foundation sources. Regardless of the particular policies and approaches the board ultimately adopts, it is essential that each new trustee is made aware of specific obligations in this area. As one presenter put it:

> If our board were not involved in fund raising, we would be out of business in a year. At least 30 percent of our contributions come from board members, and at least 60 percent of our donations are board-solicited. In addition, for big projects or in the case of unexpected financial reversals, we ask the board for special help. If the staff does not have this kind of support from its trustees, it becomes severely handicapped in its activities.

Finally, it is essential to keep in mind that the board of trustees is the ultimate authority, legally speaking, on all decisions affecting the corporation it serves. In most cases, the trustees' authority is delegated to the staff, who then carry out the organization's daily operations. Nevertheless, according to the corporation's bylaws, the board can rescind such delegation of authority at any time. Thus, the trustees' power is, at least theoretically, virtually absolute; any staff member who does not take an active interest in the board's activities and composition is risking a great deal, both personally and in relation to the future activities of the organization.

RULE 4

Give your board a WORKING STRUCTURE.

In addition to strong officers, you need a well-defined committee structure to carry out the important work of the corporation.

The full board of trustees must meet at least once a year at the corporation's annual meeting. Most boards meet at least four and as many as twelve times a year. But the real work of the board will not be carried out when so many people gather together for discussion and decision-making. Rather, most of the work will be carried out when small subdivisions of the board form committees to research and undertake specific tasks assigned to them. Usually, every member of the board will be asked to serve on at least one committee.

The committee structure has become the butt of many jokes because, all too often, it becomes so complex and overextended that one committee undermines the work of another. Communication breaks down, and the coherence of the work effort is reduced. However, effective committee organization can usually be maintained when administrative direction is strong. This is one reason why the office of president of the board of trustees is such a critical position. Given a strong, well-organized president, one who supervises and requires periodic reporting from the committees, the corporation can usually maintain excellent cohesion and internal organization. Do not, therefore, elect a board president on any but the most pragmatic grounds. Find the strongest candidate for the job. If you feel you must recognize a particular person's contribution to the organization but the person is clearly unqualified administratively for the president's job, you have the alternative of appointing an honorary president.

Like the president, the treasurer and the secretary of the corporation must be chosen carefully with specific qualifications in mind. The treasurer will be responsible for making the financial reports to the board (and, in certain instances, to state and federal agencies). In some organizations, the treasurer may be expected to sign checks, arrange for audits, assist in budget preparation, and keep tabs on the staff's

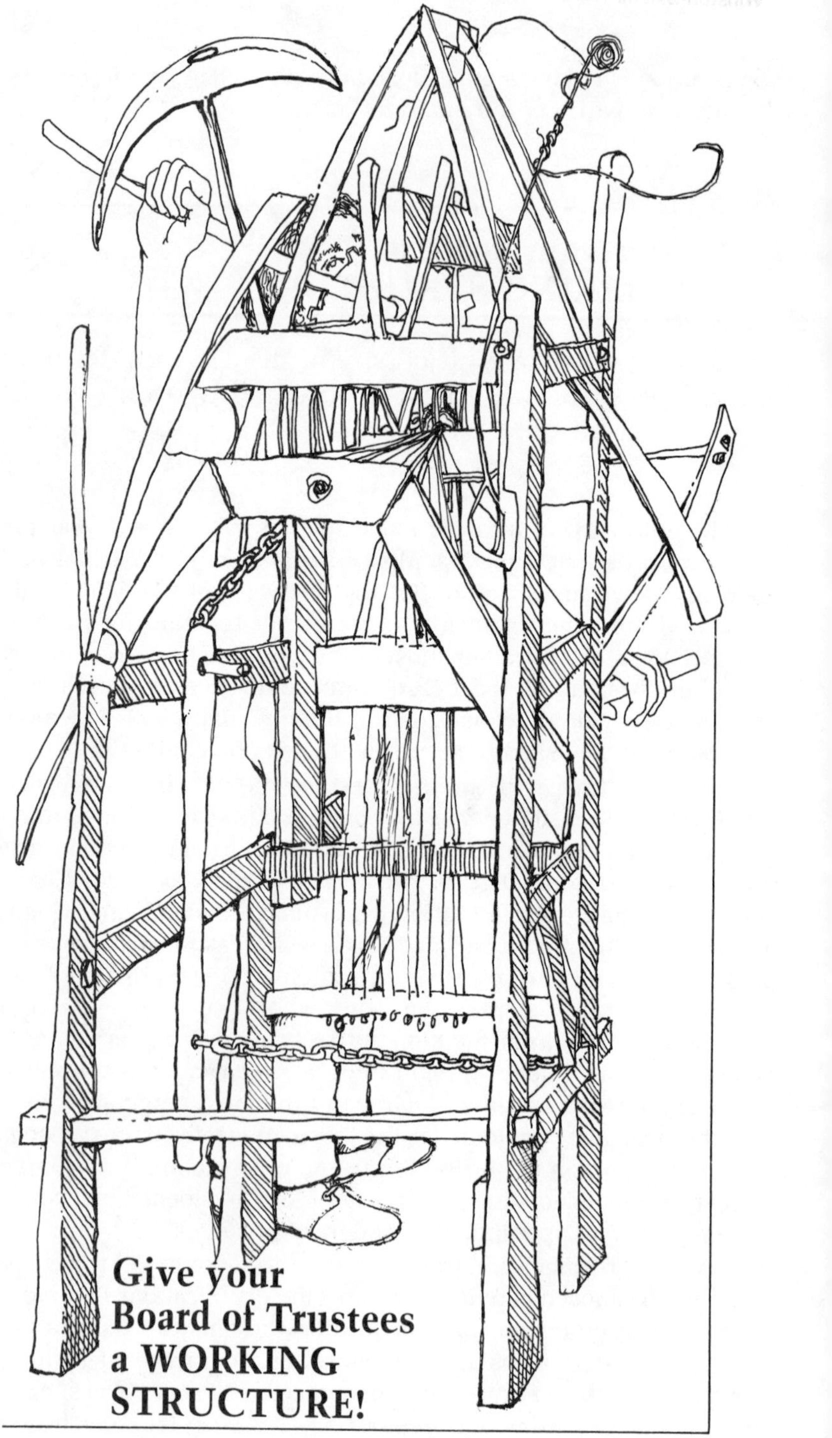
Give your
Board of Trustees
a WORKING
STRUCTURE!

use of money. Obviously, someone with financial expertise is needed in this job. The secretary of the corporation must keep accurate records of meetings, circulate minutes, send out official notification of upcoming meetings, and certify specific resolutions of the board. A well-organized person is needed for this job, one who will prepare the written records in a timely manner. Often a staff person serves in this capacity *ex officio.*

Among the committees, the one charged with the greatest administrative responsibility is the executive committee. Members of this committee include the officers of the corporation and other trustees concerned with the organization's business and fiscal affairs. It is important to keep this committee small enough so that decisions can be made quickly and easily. In fact, one of its major purposes is to avoid the necessity of convening the entire board every time a trustee decision is called for. The full board delegates its authority to the executive committee, which then becomes an extremely powerful decision-making body. Because of this, members of this committee must go out of their way to make other board members feel useful and needed. The best way to accomplish this is to give each board member a responsible job on another committee.

Most other committees are organized for specific purposes: finance, fund raising, marketing, nominating, facility, education, long-range planning, and so forth. Generally a committee is chaired by a trustee, although in many organizations other volunteers are invited to serve on the committee (except on the executive committee). This is a good way to involve more people, to spread the work load, and to assess the abilities and commitment level of prospective trustees.

At a recent conference, an arts administrator commented on the need for a committee structure:

> When I took over my organization fifteen years ago, I had to run around worrying about the maintenance of the building, approaching local businesses for donations, and reviewing the work of the auditor. I was overextended! Today things are different; I do not do any of the tasks. They are all done by committee members.

RULE 5

MAXIMIZE your work force.

When it comes to hiring staff, arts organizations find themselves in a dilemma. Money, particularly money for administration, is always in short supply—and qualified employees are expensive. The best candidates for arts administration posts are people with strong backgrounds both in the arts and in business; but if these candidates are very good, they are usually able to market themselves effectively into well-paying jobs.

Some community-based presenting organizations are staffed entirely by volunteers. However, in the majority of cases, presenters in the 1990s are finding that at least one paid administrator is necessary. Some of the most successful organizations have additional part-time or full-time staff and a large core of volunteers. Garnering the necessary skills of these individuals in a cost-efficient manner is a special kind of challenge.

Paid staff may be hired on a salaried or on a contractual basis. Salaried employees generally work fairly predictable and regular hours in a permanent capacity. Because of their status as employees, they should be given specific job descriptions which delineate their tasks, areas of responsibility, reporting lines, and so on. They can be expected to meet a specific performance standard, demonstrate commitment and responsibility, and respond to the needs of the organization. These traits are all desirable, of course, but salaried staff require an ongoing financial commitment which is likely to increase over time. Further, an organization is required to pay benefits (at the very least, workers compensation and social security), withhold tax payments, and undertake fairly detailed record-keeping (as discussed later in the chapter).

For specific or nonrecurring tasks, an organization can hire independent contractors, who are paid a fee for a specific job to be carried out over a predetermined period of time. Often, marketing and promotional needs, accounting, technical production, and specific management functions, such as planning and fund raising, can be obtained on what is called a *contractual* basis. Temporary employees, such as part-time clerical help, can also be hired in this manner. No benefits are paid, and far less paperwork is required by the IRS. However, when the majority of the individuals who work for the organization are hired on contract, there tends to be less continuity. Also, in many cases, individuals who have a continuing relationship with an organization may not legally be hired on a contractual basis.

Several decades ago, unpaid volunteers did most of the arts administration work in this country. Since then, the nature of volunteer work has changed, due in part to the professionalization of arts administrators and to the changing lifestyle of the population. Today, it is not unusual to find that the majority of volunteers for an organization are working professionals with fewer hours to spare but a high level of skills to offer. This means that presenting organizations may find themselves having to hire more help for routine jobs but being able to secure the services of high-level professionals for special projects at no cost.

MAXIMIZE
your work force.

Spend your dollars where they COUNT.

Because volunteers still do much work for presenting organizations, a major task of the presenting organization is to recruit, train, and motivate people willing to serve in this role. Often, a professional staff works closely with volunteers on such tasks as selling tickets, fund raising, meeting and entertaining performers, training ushers, and arranging and putting on special events. Occasionally, a volunteer may donate legal assistance, consulting help, financial management, or catering services. Most organizations could not make do without volunteers, and it is important to cultivate a large group of hard-working people who believe enough in your activities to lend a helping hand. However, remember that "a volunteer is an employee who cannot be fired" and choose your volunteers carefully, matching the proper person with the right job.

RULE 6

Spend your dollars where they COUNT.

Nothing gives a young administrator more of a thrill than taking over an office. Nonetheless, some of the most successful administrators work out of basements or in converted bedrooms. By choosing to work at home, administrators do a service both to their organizations and to themselves: the organizations save money on rent, and the administrators are eligible for tax deductions on their home offices although IRS guidelines have become stricter in recent years and it is well to seek advice on rules and regulations. It is true that for some people an office away from home is a necessity, because there are too many distractions at home. In that case, the organization should make a concerted effort to find donated or low-cost office space.

Low-cost or free office space is only one of many ways to save money. Nonprofit organizations that do a large amount of direct mailing can reduce costs by getting a nonprofit, bulk-rate mailing permit from the post office. In a city, you can call the "Mailing Requirements" section at the central post office to request an application; in rural areas, you can request the permit from your local post office. You will submit an initial application and then pay an annual fee, which will make the organization eligible to do an unlimited number of bulk mailings for less than half the cost of first-class mail. Each time you use bulk mail, you need to have a minimum number of pieces (or a minimum weight), and the pieces have to be presorted by zip code. But the savings can be significant if you do a number of large mailings each year.

Developing or purchasing mailing lists can be expensive, and here again there may be a way to save money. Find out whether other

KNOW the LAW.

organizations in your area have lists you can purchase or barter for. Some may provide you with mailing labels containing the names and addresses of would-be ticket buyers. The cost of the labels is modest, and because the organization probably updates the names and addresses regularly, the list itself is quite valuable. A number of community organizations may be interested in pooling their mailing lists with yours. If your list has been well maintained and is up-to-date, it is a valuable asset which can be used as barter. If you would prefer not to circulate it or if other organizations do not see your list as valuable to their interests, you can nevertheless offer to purchase their lists for a modest sum.

Various office machines are critical to maximizing income. The most obvious is a phone-answering machine, which allows a ticket buyer to leave his or her name and phone number when you are not around to take an order. It also allows you to get important messages from performers who may be in transit or need essential information. For example, performers may need to let you know of a last-minute change in travel plans that will require your picking them up in a different location if they are to get to the performance on time.

Computers are increasingly affordable labor-saving devices that save money in numerous ways. For example, a computer allows you to produce a professional-looking letter, correcting it many times, without the help of a well-trained secretary. An alphabetized mailing list on a computer can be automatically resorted by zip code to facilitate bulk mailings. Fund-raising letters can be personalized automatically by using a "mail merge" feature. More sophisticated computers with "desktop publishing" software allow presenters to do much of their own design for newsletters, programs, and the like. In thinking about purchasing a computer, you should beware the friend who offers old or used equipment. Much old equipment is out-of-date, difficult to service, and unable to handle the tasks that inexpensive new machines are designed to do. Purchasing computer hardware and software requires great expertise, and it always useful to have an experienced data-processing professional advising you once he or she has fully diagnosed your needs.

RULE 7

KNOW the LAW.

If you want to avoid ulcers and headaches, become familiar with the laws governing withholding, unemployment, copyright, and other requirements. In addition, keep a calendar with entries indicating when various state and federal forms must be filed.

Every organization must meet certain obligations to its employees; to federal, state, and local governments; and to specific private organizations. As already noted, an organization with salaried employees must withhold taxes from their paychecks, pay social security and workers compensation, and, in some cases, provide unemployment insurance. In the case of nonprofit organizations, corporate tax returns and other forms must be filed annually. If presenters know what their obligations are and if they are careful to meet all of them on time, they can avoid numerous problems; in some cases, they can also save money.

OBLIGATIONS TOWARD EMPLOYEES AND INDEPENDENT CONTRACTORS

When an organization has employees for whom it dictates specified working hours, days off, vacations, and so forth, each salaried employee must fill out a W-4 Form claiming the number of exemptions he or she is entitled to. Each pay period, the organization withholds taxes from the employee's salary. The amounts deducted are computed with the aid of tables contained in the IRS's Circular E and in publications from the state or local taxing authority. These taxes must be deposited by specific dates, ranging from four times each month to quarterly, depending on the amount to be remitted. At the same time and on the same form, the organization must report the amount of social security (or FICA) and Medicare taxes that have been paid (this obligation is shared equally by employer and employee). The employer's share of social security/Medicare is a percentage above and beyond the employee's salary and must be planned for when the organization is establishing salary levels.

Withheld taxes and social security payments are usually deposited at a commercial bank. It is absolutely essential that the deposits are made on time. Strict fines are imposed for late payments. All too often, an organization has spent the money on some other pressing financial commitment and cannot come up with the needed cash before the deadline. If your organization finds itself in this position, it is best to borrow the money and to pay on time. Quarterly, Form 941 must be filed with the IRS, reporting salaries paid, amounts withheld, and tax payments made.

The earnings of salaried employees for the previous year must be reported to the government by the end of January. A W-2 Form is used for this purpose. This form allows the organization to show how much was paid to the employee, how much social security and Medicare was paid by the employer, and how much was deducted for tax payments. One copy goes to the employee, one to the IRS, and one to the state taxing authority.

Though independent contractors and consultants do not have to have money withheld and though social security is not involved in their compensation, there are still important reporting requirements. The individuals are paid a fee (it is essential not to call it a salary). If an independent contractor earns more than $600 in a particular calendar year, the organization is obligated to report these earnings to the IRS on Form 1099. This form can be obtained from the IRS or from a local bank or post office. It should be filled out after January 1, with one copy going to the employee and another to the IRS.

Nonprofit corporations are exempt from paying federal unemployment taxes, but their obligation to pay state unemployment taxes (or state unemployment "insurance") varies state by state. In some states, organizations are required to pay a percentage of all salaries up to a specified limit. In other states, organizations have an option: they may pay state unemployment insurance so the state will cover employees that are laid off or, if they elect not to participate, they assume the risk of paying those claims themselves. Before making a final decision on this matter, you should know the law of the state and seek the advice of a knowledgeable accountant.

OTHER ACCOUNTING OBLIGATIONS

Nonprofit corporations that have more than $25,000 of gross receipts in any year are required to file a Form 990EZ or Form 990 with the IRS. This form must be filed no later than the fifteenth day of the fifth month after the annual accounting period ends. Fines for filing late are steep, though extensions may be requested for up to six months, provided a Form 2758 is filed before the normal deadline.

Because Form 990 is essentially an accounting document, it is wise to consider having it prepared by an accountant or by someone with accounting training.

The services of a CPA can be expensive, and it is generally unnecessary to hire one unless the accounting records of the organization need to be audited. Some states and many funders will require an audited or otherwise certified financial statement from any organization with gross revenues in excess of a specified amount. Although audits are useful documents, unaudited financial statements will often satisfy a small organization's needs. Audits, compilations, and reviews are different names for various kinds of outside examination of your books. Get good financial advice before deciding which, if any, of these options to choose.

A CPA's fee will usually depend on the scope of what he or she is being asked to do. All organizations should clarify in advance the basis for computing the fee as well as the extent of the services to be provided. Much of the cost of an accountant's services can be avoided if the organization has had the foresight to place a CPA on the board. The audit or independent review must be carried out by an independent CPA, one not serving on the board; but the preparation of the books for audit purposes can be done by a board member and can save considerably on the fee.

OTHER LEGAL OBLIGATIONS

There are other legal obligations that presenters should know about, because ignorance can be costly. Indeed, if financial obligations are not met in a timely manner, presenters can be liable for unpaid amounts, interest, and penalties.

COPYRIGHT LAW. All presenting organizations are required to pay music licensing fees which go to composers and other creators of concert music if their presentations involve music that is not in the public domain (generally, this is twentieth-century work). Three organizations—American Society of Composers and Publishers (ASCAP), Broadcast Music Incorporated (BMI), and Society of European Stage Authors and Composers (SESAC, Inc.)—can impose annual fees on presenters based on seating capacity and ticket price. Generally, one or more of these organizations will send a licensing contract, which will be followed by a bill once the contract is executed. For small presenters, these fees can run $300 or less per season.

LOCAL TAXES. Just because an organization is declared tax-exempt by the IRS does not mean that it is exempt from all taxes. Local entertainment taxes, excise taxes, local property taxes, and federal unrelated business income taxes are sometimes imposed. Again, the advice of a knowledgeable accountant is invaluable in determining whether an organization is subject to specific taxes and how much it should anticipate paying.

REQUIREMENTS FOR THE DISABLED. With the passage of the Americans with Disabilities Act in 1991, all public facilities must be accessible to the disabled. This is an especially important issue for presenters who own their own facilities. The National Endowment for the Arts' Office of Special Constituencies (Washington, DC 20506) can provide up-to-date information on federal regulations relating to this issue.

STATE REPORTS. Finally, most nonprofit corporations are obligated to file an annual report with the Secretary of State's office in their home state. This report details changes in trustees and officers. If you are unclear about whether this is a requirement in your state, call the appropriate agency and find out what form, if any, needs to be filed. At the same time, check with the state Attorney General's office. In some cases a state form similar to Form 990 must be filed.

RULE 8

When it comes to money, BE CAUTIOUS.

Design your budgets carefully. Be well organized in your bookkeeping and make sure that financial transactions are reviewed periodically by a member of the board.

Nothing is more important in the administration of a nonprofit organization than proper fiscal management. Unfortunately, this area is treated too casually by many arts organizations, with some people feeling that goodwill can make up for disorganization. But the pitfalls of sloppy financial management are many: lost credit, lawsuits, and even IRS review of tax-exempt status. Fund raising from public and private sources becomes more difficult if the fiscal credibility of an organization is in doubt. Keep in mind that management of the financial affairs of even a small nonprofit corporation is very different from handling your personal finances. You can probably get away with not balancing your checkbook, not keeping careful records, or not planning a budget; where your personal finances are concerned, no one is likely to bother you. But if you are as casual about the financial affairs of your organization, be prepared for trouble.

One of the most important activities of a presenting organization is budgetary planning. To project a budget, you must have a good deal of information at hand concerning anticipated expenses and income. In addition, it is extremely useful to have actual financial reports from previous years or budgets from similar kinds of organizations for reference. These will help you identify financial trends and predict income

When it comes to money, BE CAUTIOUS!

Figure 1.
BUDGET FOR UTOPIA PERFORMING ARTS SERIES

	Last Year Actual	Current Budget	Next Year Budget
INCOME			
Tickets sales	$ 42,231	$ 43,000	$ 48,000
Residency services fees	10,500	11,650	12,000
Contributions			
Individuals	28,640	30,000	32,000
Businesses	11,500	12,000	14,000
Foundations	4,500	3,500	3,500
Grants			
National Endowment	5,000	5,000	5,000
State Arts Agency	3,200	4,000	9,500
Fund-raising event	7,921	7,500	7,500
Concessions	3,226	3,000	4,000
Interest Income	7,399	8,000	8,500
TOTAL	$124,117	$127,650	$144,000
EXPENSE			
Artist fees	$ 51,200	$ 53,400	$ 62,500
Director salary/benefits	23,721	$ 24,000	25,500
Box office assistant	14,998	15,000	16,000
Advertising	8,720	9,000	10,000
Printing	6,950	7,000	7,500
Postage/supplies	3,200	3,700	4,000
Telephone	1,099	1,200	1,400
Insurance	3,750	4,000	4,500
Audit	2,500	2,500	3,000
Hall rental	4,200	4,500	5,000
License fees	600	600	600
Other/contingency	730	2,700	4,000
TOTAL	$121,668	$127,600	$144,000
SURPLUS/(Deficit)	$ 2,449	0	0

and expenditure in each budget category. Figure 1 (above) shows how a proposed budget for the coming year should be lined up next to the budget projections for the current year and the actual revenue and expenses from the previous year. For anyone looking at the proposed budget column, the dollar projections for any specific category can be checked against analogous numbers from the same category in other columns to see whether they seem reasonable. Any excessive increases or decreases must be justified. In the budget laid out in figure 1, for example, there is a substantial increase in both total income and total expense. However, the executive director was able to justify this increase by demonstrating that the organization had already received notification of a larger grant from the state arts agency and that two additional events scheduled for the season would bring in more ticket sales revenue (and add substantially to the artist fee expense).

It is always wise to be realistic but conservative in budget projections. The temptation is to exaggerate anticipated income so that more cash will be available. The inexperienced person will often justify this action by thinking, if the receipts are not forthcoming, I can always cut expenses. Besides, I am not allowed to show a profit anyway, so it really doesn't matter if we lose a little money.

This kind of thinking is dangerous and shows a fundamental misunderstanding of the nonprofit concept. First, it is difficult to cut spending when one is already well into a season. In most cases, monies are committed long ahead of the time when receipts come in. More importantly, it is essential that the presenter think in terms of building up a surplus in good years for reversals in bad. The surplus is not considered a profit so long as board members are not personally enriched by taking the surplus in the form of cash dividends. If the organization plows the surplus directly back into its programs or puts it away in a contingency fund for eventual capital expenditures or program activities, a surplus is not only legal, but desirable. An excellent goal is to project modest surpluses each year, until such time as the organization is a full season ahead in receipts and cash on hand. A healthy presenting organization is one in which there is enough cash in the bank so that an entire season could take place without income of any kind.

Why preach such fiscal conservatism? Anyone who has seen the devastating effect of rising costs or declining revenue in the past few years knows that many presenting organizations operating "close to the wire," with nothing put away for contingencies, have disappeared. In addition, growth and development are often possible only when organizations have capital put away for major acquisitions and expenditures (for example, the renovation of a building or the purchase of a new piano). Many private foundations and public agencies will not commit funds to new projects unless the organization can show a substantial "match" from its own coffers. Thus, in a very real sense, on-hand capital attracts money not only in the form of interest on savings but also in the form of grants and gifts.

Once a budget is approved, the board is faced with the question of implementation. Who signs checks? Who keeps the books? What mechanism is in place for monitoring and reviewing the fiscal management? Who makes sure that the monies are being handled legally and properly? Many presenting organizations are entirely too casual about such questions. Often an inexperienced administrator with no particular expertise in fiscal management is turned loose with the organization's checkbook. Even with the most well-meaning people, such a procedure can be disastrous. No one may be able to account for a certain sum of money that has become "lost"; cost overruns in certain categories of the budget may occur without anyone's being aware that things are amiss. With less scrupulous administrators, the temptation to "borrow" some of the organization's funds may lead to irregularities that cannot be detected or corrected.

In most well-run presenting organizations, at least two people are concerned with fiscal management. One of these is the treasurer of the corporation; the other, a senior staff person. It is primarily the treasurer who represents the board's fiduciary responsibility and assumes the ultimate responsibility for the proper handling of the organization's money. In some cases, the treasurer may exercise this authority by signing checks. Check-signing permits a convenient review of financial transactions and allows the treasurer the opportunity to verify that the staff person does not overspend in any budget category without board approval. It is generally the staff person who decides how the organization's budgeted monies are to be spent, and this person must supply the treasurer with a list of bills to be paid. In many other organizations, the staff person is given the responsibility of signing checks, although for very large checks, it may be prudent to require two signatures. If that is the case, it is necessary for the treasurer to provide some kind of regular review of the books. In no case, should one person approve payments, write checks, and review the fiscal activities of the corporation. There are simply too many risks involved, both legal and financial.

In the event that the treasurer signs checks and the director provides the approved invoices to be paid, the following procedure is quite efficient. The organization invests in a rubber stamp as below:

DATE RECEIVED ______________________
DATE PAID ______________________
ACCOUNT ______________________
CHECK # ______________________
APPROVED ______________________

When a bill is received, the staff person stamps it and fills in the first, third, and fifth lines. The first line indicates the date the invoice was received; the third line, the account (or line-item of the budget) to which the payment should be charged; on the fifth line, the staff person indicates approval by signing his or her name. The invoice is then forwarded to the treasurer for payment, and lines #2 and #4 are filled in at that time. Later, the invoice is filed to provide a "paper trail" of the transaction. In cases where no invoice or bill is received (as, for example, when performers must be paid), the director merely types a memo in the form of an invoice and treats it as such.

Two observations should be made about the person who signs the checks for the corporation. First, it is a wise precaution for this person to be bonded. Bonding is a form of insurance that protects the organization should the individual do anything improper or illegal. Second, the person who signs checks should also take responsibility for keeping up-to-date accounts of the organization's fiscal activity. The director will need to have cash-flow information and will need periodic reports—either written or oral—on amounts remaining in the various budget categories. Particularly for a director who does not see the monthly statements from the bank, some form of regular accounting from the treasurer is essential. For each line of the budget, the treasurer should indicate the total amount appropriated for the year, the amount already expended, and the amount remaining. If the volume of fiscal activity is heavy, such reports should be provided on a monthly basis. For organizations with small budgets, a quarterly or semiannual statement is usually sufficient.

Conclusion

It is difficult to exaggerate the importance of getting the administrative house of a presenting organization in order and maintaining a good, solid structure. Board and staff should consistently engage in responsible short- and long-range planning, anticipating challenges and opportunities well in advance. Planning and responsible management not only make good sense for the organization but are an important tool in fund raising. Today, funding agencies are as concerned about these issues as they are about the artistic merits of the organization. There is simply too much at stake to risk money on organizations in which administration is not taken seriously.

Many presenting organizations justify the casualness of their administrative arrangements on the basis of their small size. "With a budget of less than $25,000, we hardly have to worry about sophisticated questions of management," claimed one presenter. He may be right; one does not need a sledgehammer to pound a nail, and one probably does not have to worry about complex administrative issues when the organization's budget is so small. But remember this: no budget is too small to be managed properly. Moreover, because presenting organizations have a tendency to grow, it is just as well to start off on a sound footing that will allow for safe and well-managed development.[2]

Remember, performers are PEOPLE, too.

2

Programming and Performers

> What we put on stage is not only what the public sees, it is who we are. It tells the public what we stand for, what we wish to offer to the community, and how well we know our business. If audience members like or are impressed by what they see, they will come back. If they consistently question our judgment, they won't. Our audience doesn't have to like everything, but they must understand and respect our decisions. Our programming philosophy and our selection of performers are critical—they reflect our mission, our image, and they determine our survival!

When a presenter with thirty years of experience speaks about programming and performer selection, it is important to listen. This presenter makes an important point: programming is more than hiring performers out of a catalogue or brochures or from showcase conferences. Selecting performers is more complicated than going to the supermarket and filling a shopping cart. Programming is akin to planning an elaborate series of menus after determining the tastes of your local community. You may offer several delicacies that everyone will enjoy and some adventuresome offerings that no one has tasted before. In the end, you want everyone to say they enjoyed the meal.

The first step is to decide what kinds of events and artists you want to include in your programs. Are you going to limit yourself to a single discipline, such as theater or modern dance, or are you going to offer several? Are you going to be presenting styles with which community members are familiar, or are you planning to program works that will be uncharted territory?

Once you have established a broad programming philosophy, you have to find affordable performers who will make the community celebrate your choices, or at least respect them. Indeed, that is what this chapter is all about. Many first-time presenters believe that hiring performers is essentially a business transaction. Although there are certainly business elements in working with performers, the best presenters look on their dealings with performers and their agents as a collaboration that will serve the wishes and needs of both parties and, ultimately, the community.

RULE 9

Remember, performers are PEOPLE, too.

Señor Pizzicato, the orchestra conductor in the children's classic *Tubby the Tuba*, is the perfect example of what many people still believe to be the typical performer personality. Aloof, exalted, authoritarian, his accent and foreign origin the very essence of "culture," Señor Pizzicato moderates his austere personality only when meeting people whose musical sensitivity begins to approach his own. We are to be impressed and a little fearful of the maestro, just as we are to be a bit subservient in our dealings with any artist who has chosen to share his or her performing talents with us.

Unfortunately, the myth of the exalted performer—so charmingly stereotyped for kids in *Tubby the Tuba*—is firmly believed by many people who must deal with performers on a regular basis. Some performers do foster this image. In certain instances, however, they have been forced to adopt a selfish or arrogant attitude by the insensitivity of audiences and presenters. "How can I be generous and courteous," asks one, "when on the day of the performance the presenter keeps phoning, not letting me get any sleep?" "Of course I left the after-concert reception," says another. "I was famished. I hadn't eaten anything before the concert, and all I was offered were some packaged cookies and punch." "I didn't want to appear high-handed," says a third, "but when someone asked me to play the theme from *Star Wars* during intermission, I asked him to leave the backstage area so I could practice." "Six weeks after the performance, when I still hadn't received a check," says a fourth, "I called the presenter and got angry. He didn't seem to realize that I had bills to pay, too."

But the fault is not entirely on the side of presenters and audiences. Performers often exploit the idea that creative people need not fulfill normal obligations or maintain minimal levels of courtesy. Some performers break contracts, occasionally only days before a performance. Others fail to send promotional materials in time to be useful. Still others send a description of the program several weeks ahead, allow this material to be advertised, and then show up with an entirely different program. In addition, presenters are often expected to suffer quietly when performers make unreasonable demands for their own personal comfort, are tardy for performances, and are rude to members of the audience or board. In many cases, presenters feel themselves to be in an extremely vulnerable position. After all, a performance is at stake, and they want to do everything in their power to make that performance a success. Nor are they always certain what demands are reasonable. On the theory that it is better to be taken advantage of than to be discourteous, presenters often give in when they should not.

Mythology needs to be replaced with reality, and one theme must consistently be stressed: performers are people, too. This means that they must be treated like people and must be held responsible like people.

RULE 10

DON'T buy a pig in a poke.

Hiring performers is a tricky business. One must first attempt to find out how good they are artistically; then one must try to determine whether they are reliable, courteous, and easy to work with. Even if all these things check out, the question remains whether the group will please the audience. If the performers are doing a residency that includes several services in various locations, the questions multiply. How effective are the performers with different types of audience groups? Do they work effectively with children? Are they comfortable in informal settings? Are they willing to go into less-than-ideal perform-

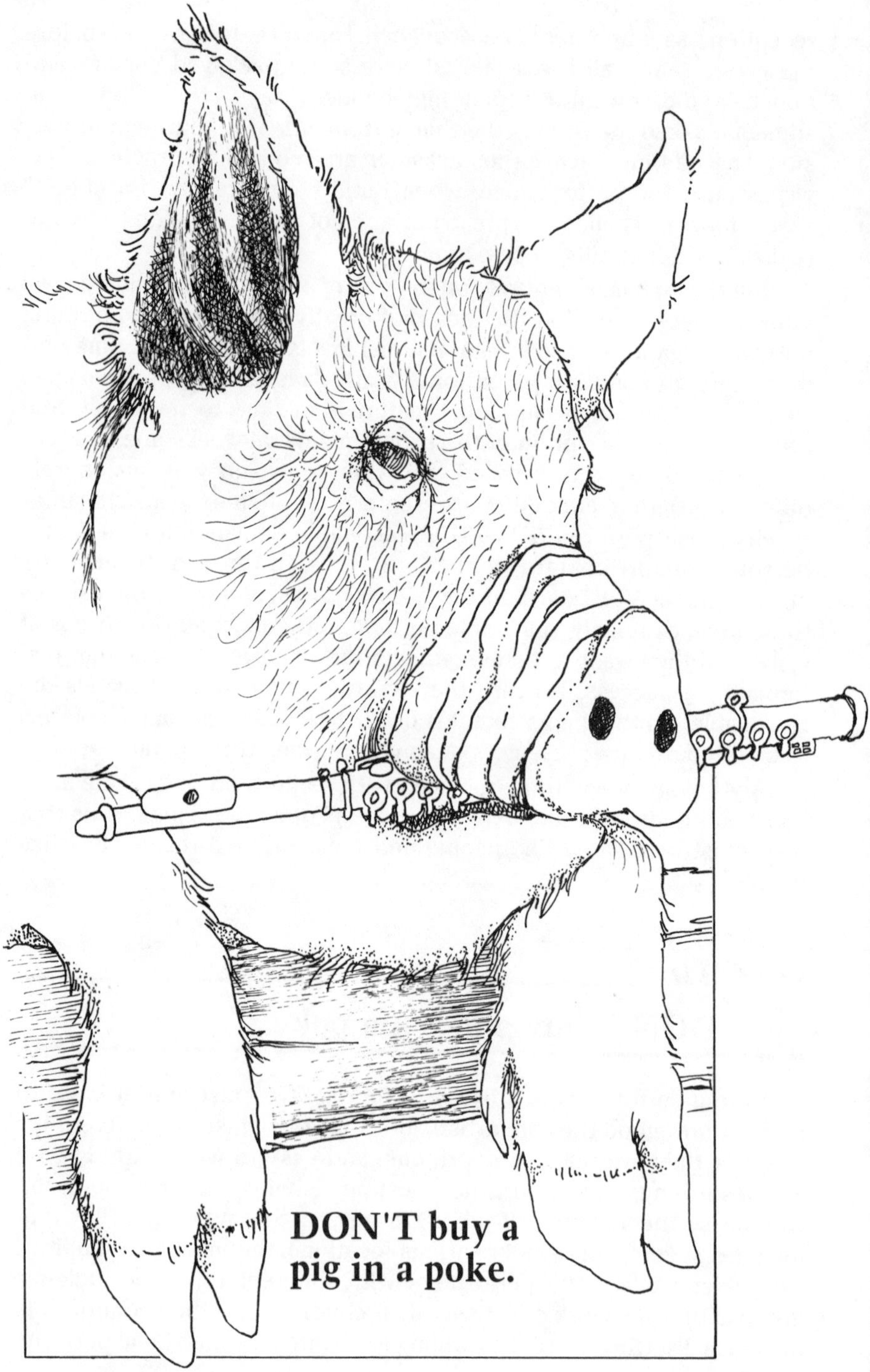

DON'T buy a pig in a poke.

ing spaces? Are they adaptable and flexible? Will they be effective "missionaries" for the arts? Will they be courteous?

How can a presenter learn the answers to all these questions? One way is to ask a lot of questions. Some performers represent themselves; others are represented by booking agents and managers. These sources are always the best place to start. Artists or their representatives should be able to supply you with biographical information about the performers, program and repertoire, and places where the artists have performed, as well as sample records and tapes, and other promotional materials. It is important to remember, however, that the purpose of promotional materials is to sell; thus, they always present artists in the best possible light. Even reviews and letters of support are undependable. A performing group may be using in 1995 an impressive review that was written in 1975. Obviously, much may have changed in the intervening years, but the banner review is still used to entice the presenter.

The best way to judge performers is to see or hear them in action. Some state and regional arts agencies and some presenter service organizations now provide travel assistance for this purpose. Get a list of the group's performing dates, find the ones closest to your community, and try to attend at least one event. If your presenting plans include a residency, try to attend at least one workshop, clinic, master class, or performance for children. Have the performers made an effort to design something appropriate in their residency events or have they simply diluted their formal show? Judge the audience reaction objectively, regardless of whether you personally like the group. If you like what you see, talk to the presenter. Has the group been prompt for performances? Have the performers been courteous and easy to work with? Have there been any special problems? Ask the presenter how much he or she paid for the group. This information may turn out to be important when you start your own negotiations.

In the past few years, presenters have formed state and regional consortia. These networks are an invaluable source of information about performers. Many of the organizations present booking conferences, which offer their members and others a chance to meet with agents and sometimes with the performers themselves. These are also excellent opportunities to meet with other presenters who have worked with specific groups you are considering. For more information on these consortia, you should call your state or regional arts agency.

Suppose you do not have time to attend many performances, but you can spare a day or two to see several. If you are lucky, there may be a showcase of performing groups in your area in which several performers are doing short segments of their work for potential presenters. One way to find out when special showcases are taking place is to write or call your state arts agency; in addition to providing information, state arts agencies often sponsor or co-sponsor showcases themselves.

The disadvantage of a showcase is that it is an artificial situation geared toward selling. Often the location is technically incompatible with the needs of the performing group. The presentation is generally short—twenty minutes or less—so it is difficult for the performers to demonstrate what they can do. Also, a showcase is rarely an actual performance before a regular audience, so it is difficult to gauge audience response. The best showcases attempt to correct this defect by bringing in audiences. One children's theater showcase in Vermont, for example, took place in a regional high school. Children were brought in from surrounding elementary schools. Thus, the presenters in the audience had a chance to assess how successful the performing groups were with children of various ages.

Regardless of whether you attend a showcase, it is always desirable to speak to presenters who have hired the performing group you are considering. Ask the booking agent or representative to send you a list of organizations that the group has performed for in the past two years, with the name, address, and phone number of each presenter. Even if the performing group does not send you a complete list and manages to delete the presenters who would give you the most negative evaluations, you will still receive much valuable information from presenters who were pleased, on the whole, with the group's work. You will be told what to watch out for, what to insist upon, how much to pay, and other details that will help you not only in making the initial decision but also in dealing with the group later on.

Do not underestimate the importance of performer selection. The reputation of your organization is at stake every time you choose performers. If the group you have chosen presents a mediocre performance, the audience will believe that your organization lacks people with expertise and good judgment. No matter what the previous track record of the organization, one fiasco can do considerable harm, especially to a young presenting organization's reputation. So be careful and take the necessary steps to be sure you are buying quality.

Finally, if you have success with certain performers, do not be afraid to hire them again. Reengaging performers gives your audience members a chance to watch them mature; it also offers the audience an opportunity to welcome back old friends. Further, audiences are frequently more willing to hear and see unfamiliar work when it is performed by an artist or an ensemble that they know and trust. If you are worried about variety, skip a season before reengaging a group;

but remember that many performers vary their presentations from year to year anyway. The finest performing groups—those that have built a solid reputation in the field of touring—usually depend on reengagements for 50-75 percent of their bookings. This is hardly surprising. Reliability and a good track record are precisely what the experienced presenter is usually looking for.

RULE ***11***

It's often NEGOTIABLE.

The price of a performing group, like the price of a car, can usually be negotiated. Attempt to block-book or arrange a residency and you may be able to get more services for fewer dollars.

If you go to a department store to buy a piece of furniture or an article of clothing, you do not expect to haggle about prices. Occasionally a desired item may be on sale, but you, the purchaser, had little to do with the markdown. Shopping in a department store is a take-it-or-leave-it situation. Either you buy at the price marked or you do not buy at all.

Although there are a handful of star performers or performing groups who fit into the "take-it-or-leave-it" category, most do not; and prices are often adjusted to accommodate special and not-so-special situations. Most performers have a stated fee, but this is often open to negotiation. Presenters should investigate carefully and perhaps bargain a bit before agreeing on a price.

The situation in which a performing group is least likely to lower its fee is when a presenting organization wants to hire the group for a single performance in a geographically isolated area. When much travel is necessary and only a single fee is in the offing, the performing group may be unable to lower its fee without losing money. However, the same presenter who finds that a group's booking agent is firm about the price for a single performance may find a changed attitude if several performances are possible. After all, the group must realize a certain amount to cover its touring expenses. The fewer engagements that can be secured, the higher will be the fee for each engagement. Conversely, a tightly booked tour with many performances allows everyone to enjoy financial benefits—the performers and their representatives earn more, the presenters save more.

It's often NEGOTIABLE.

There are two methods of arranging multiple performances: the block-book and the residency. To block-book, two or more presenters in the same geographical area cooperate in hiring a performing group. If one presenter books the group on Monday, the second might sign them up for Tuesday. If, in addition, one of the presenters agrees to house and feed the performers, the fee is lowered by a greater amount. Because the block-booking format can realize some savings, presenting organizations in many parts of the country have developed formal or informal consortia. The members of a consortium cooperate in planning their respective seasons, sharing some performers when this fits in with their overall artistic goals. When they are ready to negotiate with the performing group by offering multiple bookings, they may be able to secure lower fees.

Some consortia are formal organizations with paid professional staff serving a large membership. But many are simply loose affiliations of presenters who realize the same benefits simply by keeping in touch by phone with other presenting organizations in their area. Said one arts administrator: "Once you pick up the phone and call a colleague about his or her plans for the coming season, you have a consortium." The best way to find out more about potential cooperating presenters in your area is to get in touch with the regional arts organization in your area (see appendix G). These organizations maintain computerized lists which show not only the geographic location of presenters but their programming patterns, budget size, and other useful information.

The second method of arranging multiple performances is to organize a residency. The purpose of a residency is to expose the community more broadly and completely to the performing arts. When a performing group does a residency, the performers come into an area for a certain period of time, usually two to five days but sometimes much longer. They give several formal and informal presentations in various community locations, including schools, civic clubs, radio stations, community centers, senior citizen residences, and concert halls. Ultimately, such residencies contribute to broader participation in the arts and the development of arts audiences.

From a financial point of view, the more extensive services and the broader goals of a residency often justify its greater cost. There are savings to be realized here as well. The longer the performing group stays, the lower the cost per day. For example, one classical music duo in New England charges $1,000 for a single performance but only $700/day for a four-day residency, which includes three services each day. The savings are dramatic if the presenting organization can find other co-presenters to help defray the total cost of the residency program.

Obviously, if you decide to organize a residency, you must choose the performing group carefully. Many performers who do marvelous work in a concert hall or theater do poor residencies. They may be unsuccessful with children or with others who are inexperienced attenders of arts events. They may be stand-offish in informal settings and generally temperamental in situations requiring flexibility and tolerance. It is always advisable to find out, for example, what the minimum requirements for performing space will be before the group arrives. Some groups are willing to perform anywhere; others have stringent requirements. Since residency locations vary enormously and have a way of not quite turning out as expected, opt for the more flexible group.

If the presenting organization can provide hospitality—housing and meals for the performing group—during the residency, more money can be saved. Sometimes local colleges or motels will donate rooms and meals. Occasionally, private homes can be used, though many of the more experienced performers will not agree to stay with families. Whatever the arrangement, keep the following in mind. Performers need rest; if they are housed in private homes, it should be understood that they are not to be disturbed at certain hours. In addition, many performers have special eating habits. Most, for example, dislike eating a heavy dinner before a performance. Make sure that the host and hostess are aware of this and do not plan a big dinner party in honor of the invited guests—unless, of course, it is after the performances.

One hospitality system that works well with younger and more adaptable performers is to house them with families, but arrange for meal coupons to be donated by local restaurants. This allows the performers to eat when they want and what they want without being rude to the host families. Since one of the principal purposes of a residency is to break down the barriers between the performing artist and members of the community, many presenters like the arrangement of at least housing the performers in private homes.

With regard to the fees for a performing group, be straightforward with booking agents when you talk with them. If the fee for a particular group is quoted at $2,500 and you want to spend only $1,800, ask the booking agent whether there is some way that the group can meet your price. Tell him or her that your budget is fixed and you will have to book in another group if your price cannot be met. Often, compromises can be worked out: if you, for example, will be flexible about a date, the booking agent may arrange an "en route" fee when the performing group is in your area anyway. When it comes to establishing fees, presenters have a good deal of leverage—an advantage that few of them use effectively in their dealings with performing groups.

Finally, it is well to remember that, though some people find the negotiating process difficult or even intimidating, it is a unique opportunity for you to learn more about the performers and their agent and for them to learn more about you, your organization, your facility, and your community. For those presenters who stay in the field for several years, there will be frequent interactions with artists and their representatives. It is worthwhile to start these communications off on a positive footing.

RULE 12

INSIST on a contract.

A contract protects the presenter as much as it does the performing group. Always insist on one and always read it carefully before signing.

At one time, a number of presenters took pride in never using contracts with the performing groups they hired. "We have a special relationship with our performers," said one presenter some years ago, "so why should we risk spoiling it by introducing something as impersonal as a contract?" This attitude was admirable but dangerous. Contracts help to spell out in writing the precise agreement between the performing group and the presenting organization. They help prevent misunderstandings or forgetfulness on the part of either signer. A contract should be regarded as a form of communication, which sets out the obligations and expectations of both parties.

Some people resist contracts because they are afraid of becoming entangled in a legally binding agreement. With most contracts, however, litigation is an option that is practically never considered. Almost no one would go to court to collect a $2,500 fee, just as no presenting organization would go to court over a change in the specified number of performers appearing on stage. Nevertheless, a contract serves as a reminder that certain agreements have been made and that either party has a claim on the other if the terms are not met. When either the presenters or the performers believe they have been shortchanged, the contract serves as a document of arbitration. Thus, if you are told by a performing group that they do not use contracts, insist on one (a sample contract is presented in appendix B). If you follow the format of contracts that have stood the test of time, you are more likely to have a trouble-free performance or residency.

INSIST on a contract.

In looking over a contract sent to you by a performing group, you should be particularly sensitive to anything that is unfamiliar or difficult to understand. Look carefully at the contract and make sure you have been sent all the "riders"—extra pages specifying additional agreements beyond those spelled out in the contract proper. Do not sign until you understand all the terms completely. Otherwise, you may be committing yourself to additional costs and responsibilities. For example, in the contract sample in appendix B, Rider B, in particular, could spell disaster for a presenter who initialed it without knowing what was involved.

In general, once a contract is signed, it should continue to be the reference point from which all discussions flow. If a disagreement arises between the presenter and the performers, the contract may provide a useful vehicle for resolution. The contract has a psychological value as well. Once people commit their names to a legal document, they are more likely to be careful in carrying out their responsibilities.

It is true that a contract can never cover every possible contingency. When something happens that is not covered by a contract, experienced groups tend to compromise. Consider the following example:

> A touring opera company was to perform on a February evening at a university town in western Massachusetts. During the day, a severe snowstorm caused the roads to ice up, and the company trailer truck, carrying the scenery, costumes, lights, and other equipment, jackknifed two miles from the theater. There was no hope of getting the truck out of the ditch until the following morning. The performers arrived safely about an hour later. The company manager quickly assessed the situation and determined that it was possible to give a performance because the essential equipment could be taken to the theater by pickup truck. Nevertheless, much of the scenery and all of the costumes, which were packed in the front of the truck's trailer, would have to be left behind. A hasty meeting was called with the presenter, who wanted to postpone the show as permitted under the *force majeure* provision of the contract. The company manager explained that this was impossible: the company was headed to the Midwest the following morning and would not return to New England during the tour. The presenter countered by saying that he was worried about the size of the audience—the snow might keep them away—and the disappointment of some who had expected to see full scenery and costumes. At this point, the manager made an offer. The company would do the show in street clothes and partial scenery; the conductor would make a special announcement before the performance

Use your performers FULLY.

> and explain the scenic situation before each act. If, at the end, the presenter felt compromised, either artistically or economically, a fair financial settlement could be worked out. The presenter somewhat reluctantly agreed.
>
> At 8:20 that evening, twenty minutes behind schedule, the performance began with a speech by the conductor to the large audience that had braved the weather to come to the show. By the end of the evening, the audience gave the performers a standing ovation. As one individual said later, "I felt that I was almost a part of the company and that the performers had made a secret pact with us that this was going to be a very special evening." After it was all over, the presenter decided not to press for any special financial settlement as long as the performing group would pay the stagehands who had appeared for work but had been sent home.

This example shows that when two experienced professionals are willing to compromise, both can turn out to be winners in what otherwise might prove to be a financially calamitous venture. In addition, it makes another point: cancellations should be avoided. In recent years, both presenters and artists have canceled all too frequently. Cancellations damage everyone's credibility, cause financial losses, and create distrust. Presenters should make sure that the contract contains some provision for financial compensation for out-of-pocket and promotional costs if a performing group cancels without cause. At the same time, presenters should always recognize that a signed contract is an obligation to present and to pay if the performers live up to their end of the bargain.

RULE 13

Use your performers FULLY.

Make good use of the performers while they are in your employ. If your organization is truly serving the community, the performers should appear in places where a variety of people can enjoy them.

One misconception associated with the mystique of the exalted performing artist is that he or she appears only on an elegant concert stage or in a theater. There is still a pervasive belief that artists should not be asked to perform in less formal settings. This belief is unfortunate because it prevents presenters from using performers in places where they might have a marked effect on appreciative audiences. Two national service organizations that have been working hard to combat this situation over the years are Young Audiences and Affiliate Artists. The former originally became famous for introducing school-age children to music; the latter, for saturating communities with informal "noncerts" or "informances," in which distinguished artists perform in every kind of location for diverse audiences.

The achievements of these organizations are considerable. However, much of what they have accomplished can also be done by small, community-based presenting organizations. Taking performers into the community entails careful planning and is certainly more complicated than having the community come to a central location, such as a concert hall or theater. Nevertheless, a series of formal performances in an auditorium may be forbidding to people who rarely attend cultural events, nor will outside funding sources be convinced that sufficiently diverse segments of the population are being served by such a series of programs. Finally, remember the mathematics of performer fees: the longer a group's period of residence, the lower the per-performance fee. If a group is in your area anyway, they will likely be willing to perform one or two extra informal services for a small additional fee.

Though cost-effective, a residency is not necessarily easy to organize. One has to know what the performers are capable of and willing to do, where they like to work, which format works best for them. One has to know one's community and have cooperating organizations that can provide volunteers or staff to assist with logistics. Planning is essential. The best residencies generally entail a good deal of discussion with the artists and the cooperating organizations, all of whom become partners in developing an overall strategy for effectively reaching a broad segment of the community.

The most obvious alternative location for performing arts events, and the one most commonly used, is a school.[3] Because schoolchildren are audiences of the future, they must be cultivated through an exposure to live performances. But presenters and performers should realize that a standard, forty-five-minute assembly program before a large group of children may not be the most effective performing format. Intensive sessions with smaller groups, or residency activities that involve repeated exposure over a period of days or weeks, should be considered. Performers who have a good deal of experience with school programs often have pre-visit materials that can go to classroom teachers to prepare for the on-site time, or post-visit materials to reinforce what has been learned. If such materials have not been developed, someone from your organization might work with teachers, performers, or both groups to help develop them. They undoubtedly will make the residency activities more meaningful.

Even on short residencies, performers can engage students in ways that capture their interest. A brass quintet might do a workshop with high school band players; a puppeteer might work with an art class on puppet construction; dancers might do a session on movement with the physical education class. Not only do these intensive sessions seem to have a longer lasting effect on children, but performers generally prefer them. They are usually more fulfilling than the more formal assembly programs, particularly those involving groups of less-than-attentive young people. Because of this, many performers will increase their daily time commitment to the presenting organization if they are working only with small groups of children (thirty or fewer). The following example provides an interesting illustration:

> The booking agent for a woodwind quintet doing a residency in a small New England city told the presenter that she could schedule the group for up to three services each day. For the first two days of the five-day residency, the presenter organized six large auditorium concerts for elementary school students in various parts of the city. After the second day, the leader of the group told the presenter that the performers preferred working with fewer children and would be willing to increase the number of services if they could work with individual classrooms. Would she be willing, he asked, to allow the members of the group to split up and make several classroom visits covering an entire school of twenty-one classrooms in a morning? The presenter agreed and decided to follow one of the musicians—the flutist—on his round of visits. In the first classroom, the performer introduced himself, played a short piece on the flute, then on the piccolo. Afterward he demonstrated the principle of changing the pitch on wind instruments by means of a Coke bottle and colored water. He asked one of the children to "tune" his Coke bottle by pouring water to the correct level. Next, the flutist took out a special screwdriver and took apart the flute's foot-joint while explaining the nature of the instrument's construction. "The instrument is like a very delicately constructed machine," he remarked, and then showed the children what was necessary to keep it in good playing order. During the short question period that followed, several children asked him questions about how instruments are put together—this in a town where many parents worked in construction trades. The flutist ended with a spirited flute solo before departing for another classroom.

In this case, though the musicians spent an entire morning in the school, the presenting organization was charged for only two services.

Although schools are the most obvious sites for residency activities, options for adult education and social-service-type residencies are limitless. Some presenters have worked effectively with continuing education divisions of local universities to develop courses that include residency activities as well as tickets to the performances. Lecture series relating to a particular art form, type of work, or artist are another possibility. Lecture demonstrations and open rehearsals are popular in many communities. Miniperformances at senior centers or local businesses often reach community members who may not attend a full-length performance in your facility. If you know your community well, you will find many opportunities for interchange between the visiting artist and community members.

In considering other community locations for performances, you would find it best to consult first with the booking agent or leader of the group to learn about the minimal requirements for performing space—for example, dancers generally require a wood floor and will not dance on cement; a renaissance chamber group cannot be heard in a large gymnasium and may request smaller performing spaces. Once you have an idea of space requirements, determine which particular audiences your organization wants to reach. If it is senior citizens, find out whether there is a community facility in which large numbers of older people tend to congregate during the week. If it is the business community, perhaps you should arrange a luncheon performance at one of the civic clubs in town, such as the Rotary. Finally, do not be afraid to schedule the performers in shopping centers, banks, factories, or anywhere else where positive exposure to the performing arts will result. Check out your local contacts carefully, however, and make sure you will receive plenty of assistance when you arrive with your group. Someone who has an official connection with the performing space should agree to share responsibility for organizing the special event—the kind of person who, for example, has the authority to turn off the electronic Muzak when your artists are ready to give a live performance. The following is an example of an unusual use of a performing group:

> A community-based presenting organization that offered several residencies in its city each year was concerned that an entire segment of the population was not being reached. An analysis of audiences revealed that except for college-affiliated individuals, almost no one in the eighteen-to-thirty-year-old age bracket was attending any of the events. After much deliberation, the program director met with an executive of a large insurance office in the city and asked whether there was any way that he might arrange a program for the

> workers in his employ, most of whom were in the desired age range. After some hesitation about the feasibility of the project, the executive suggested that an informal concert be arranged during the mid-afternoon coffee break in the cafeteria. The company, as its contribution, would make the necessary arrangements and allow the coffee break to be stretched to 35 minutes. At 3:15 on a January afternoon, more than three hundred people filed into the cafeteria, went through the coffee line, and sat quietly as they were treated to an informal performance. For many, it was their first exposure to live classical music.

In scheduling these extra performances by the group you have selected, keep in mind that there is a limit to the amount of work you can reasonably expect performers to do well. Try to schedule a block of time for performances and another one for the performers to rest. This is generally more desirable than spreading the services throughout the day. You should always find out from the booking agent just how many services you are entitled to and avoid the temptation to increase this number. If certain members of the group are especially energetic and enthusiastic and are willing to do additional short appearances on the radio or for potential contributors, you may make use of this opportunity. But never try to force performers to do more than you have hired them to do.

Occasionally you will find performers who are disdainful of performing in any facility other than a concert hall or a theater. For them, the residency format is merely a necessary evil in the difficult business of trying to make a living. Try to screen out performers of this type before you hire them for residencies; certainly make very clear, before any contract is signed, what plans you have for the group. If you have been detailed and explicit, the group should have few surprises; you, in turn, should feel you have every right to see your plans carried out.

RULE **14**

PREPARE your performers.

Be in touch with the performers well before they are expected to arrive. Anticipate any special needs. Give clear information about where they are to go and who will be there to greet them.

A trouble-free event or series of events often depends upon the effectiveness of communication between the presenter and the

PREPARE your performers.

performing group. Much important information must be exchanged before the performers arrive. If you are able, try to be in touch with artists directly, sending written information several weeks ahead confirming the date, time, and location of the performances, giving travel directions to good restaurants and to the auditorium (preferably with a map), recommending accommodations in the area with locations and room prices, and any other information relevant for the performance or residency. If the performers are staying with families, the letter should give the name of the host family where each performer is staying (including children's names), the address, and any other special information that might turn out to be useful (for example, "the Smiths' daughter, Susan, plays clarinet so I put your clarinetist with them"). In the letter, specify what time you would like the group to arrive and give the name and phone number of two individuals to be telephoned upon arrival (in case one is out, the second can serve as an alternative). Ask for any additional information relevant to the performance—for example, will music stands be required? Will the auditorium be needed for a rehearsal? Would the performers be willing to attend a reception after the event?

Ideally you will be able to communicate with the performers by mail and follow up with a telephone call to confirm that the information has been received and digested. However, many performers are on tour a great deal of the time and are not easily reachable by mail or phone. The best way to communicate in these situations is through the performers' manager/representative, although it is still highly desirable to make contact by phone directly with the performer or a representative traveling with the group, especially if technical matters need to be discussed and confirmed. This can be done by getting the itinerary of the performers. Call another presenter on the tour and ask him or her to get a message to the performers to call you at a specific time.

If a performing group is involved in a residency that has several performance locations, it will be necessary to add several items to the letter you send to the leader of the group: a master schedule with the date, time, and location of each performance; a presenter contact (person to be notified upon arrival) for each performance location; and a master map showing the location of restaurants, motels, or host family homes, and the place where each event is to occur.

One successful community-based organization that specializes in arranging residencies each year has devised the following system for preparatory materials. The usual letter is sent to the performing group's leader six weeks before the date of arrival. Then, when the group arrives, each performer gets an information packet, which includes a letter of welcome, a brochure describing the organization's residency

Be a good PARENT to your performers.

programs, an annotated map, and a listing of all essential details concerning the location and time of each performance, information on host families, local amenities and services (laundromats, exercise facilities, medical facilities, financial institutions, local restaurants open late at night). For large performing groups, the same packet of materials can be given to the company manager, who will take responsibility for getting the company to the right place at the right time.

The efforts expended on preparatory work of this kind will have a beneficial effect. With detailed information, performers are less likely to become confused about what is expected of them. Given a presenter who is on top of things and has attempted to make life a little simpler for them, performers generally go out of their way to be helpful and supportive.

RULE **15**

Be a good PARENT to your performers.

The care and feeding of performers involves a healthy mix of firmness, fairness, and consistency. Be aware of your obligations but insist on what is your due.

It is impossible to generalize about the behavior of performers. Like any large group of people, those in the performing arts display every kind of personality. Some are kind, helpful, and cooperative; others, unpleasant, self-centered, and difficult to work with. Some performers are extremely nervous; others are calm no matter what the situation. The most important thing to remember about performers is that their behavior cannot be predicted simply by their profession. A creative person may be responsible or irresponsible, organized or disorganized, sensitive or insensitive. For this reason, presenters must assess the personalities of performers on an individual basis and adjust their behavior accordingly.

There are certain things a presenter should consistently attempt to do for the performers. A performer is a guest in your community and should be met and welcomed on arrival. Presenters should make sure that the performers' schedule leaves adequate time to rest and relax; that they are encouraged to get in some recreational activities while they are in town (one traveling woodwind quintet is well known for having two members who like to work out every day in a gymnasium); that they have the opportunity to eat well according to their own desired schedule. Presenters should make sure that there is someone at every performance location to help members of the group find their way around, set up, locate rest rooms, and generally feel welcome. Someone from the presenting organization should accompany members of the group to performance locations. Many presenters do not realize that it is also important to praise a job well done. Performers need positive feedback on their work, and this is something that busy presenters tend to forget.

It is the presenter's obligation to pay the performing group promptly after the final performance or service. The contract will specify whether a check is to be given to the leader of the group at performance time or mailed to the artists' representative. Once the performing group has fulfilled its obligations to your organization, there is no reason why they should be kept waiting for payment. For many performers, a delay in payment can create difficulties with landlords, bill collectors, and the like. Similarly, performers often run short of cash on the road, and you should be prepared to help individual artists cash your organization's check at a local bank.

Presenters often assume that performers like to be entertained at parties after performances. This is often true, but not always. Some performers like to unwind after a couple of hours of hard work on stage; others are tired and want to go to bed; still others want to go off together and have a beer or a quiet evening alone. This is not to say that you should avoid after-performance entertainment—simply that you should clear your plans with the performers and never assume that they should or must come. If you do entertain them after a performance, expect them to be hungry and thirsty. Do not serve them cookies and punch, even if that is what you are giving the rest of the guests. Assume that they will want to eat a meal and feed them properly. In many cases, this will be the first real meal of the day for them.

Just as presenters should make every effort to treat performers well, they have every right to expect performers to meet their obligations to the presenting organization. Presenters should not tolerate a rude or arrogant attitude toward the audience or members of the community. Much harm can be done if the performers do not make a minimal effort to be courteous. If you observe rude behavior, speak to the people involved and explain how important it is for your organization to project a positive image in the community. Ask for their cooperation. Do not get angry but be clear about your complaint. As a general rule, tell the group that you expect them to show up at least half an hour before the scheduled time of performance. If anyone is late, wait until after the performance is over, and then speak individually to the person involved. Calmly state that you are serious about the half-hour "call" and you hope that the lateness was simply an oversight. Finally, if you are unhappy or dissatisfied with the performers after the visit, call or write the artists' representative and explain your feelings. The feedback is often much appreciated and can be extremely helpful to the performers.

Conclusion

Dealing with performers is simple as long as you can combine the wisdom of Solomon, the patience of Job, and the strength of Samson. For most of us, this is an unlikely possibility. As a result, the relationship between presenters and performers is brought off successfully only when both sides are willing to make an effort. Certainly presenters can determine to a large extent how things will go. It is presenters who initially choose performing groups, make the necessary preparatory arrangements, set up schedules, and, in general, establish the tone of the relationship. Presenters who are flighty, disorganized, unduly harsh, or ridiculously gushing will not command the respect of performers. Performers do seem to admire presenters who are well organized, concerned for their comfort, and clear about the requirements of the presenting organization.

Many performers have themselves become successful presenters. One, much respected by the performers he hires, attributes his success to an understanding of the performers' point of view. "I always try to put myself in their shoes," he says, "because I remember so clearly my own frustration with presenters. Perhaps the most important thing to keep in mind is the notion that performers have the same human qualities and frailties as the rest of us."

You have to MAKE it happen.

3

Filling the Auditorium

Nothing is quite as pathetic as an empty auditorium on a performance night. Not only is it depressing for the performers, but it usually indicates a financial calamity for the organizers of the event. Conversely, nothing is more uplifting (spiritually and financially) than a sold-out hall. There is a special kind of excitement for performers, audience, and management when all seats are filled at performance time.

Is there some magical secret that the successful manager possesses which enables him or her to sell out a hall? The secret of successful selling, simply stated, is hard work—forever. Though some people believe that hiring a big-name attraction or performer will ensure large crowds, this is not necessarily the case. I remember a story my grandmother used to tell about attending a concert in Florida featuring the legendary Jascha Heifetz; there were only 27 people in a 3,000-seat auditorium. Big names can certainly make the job of selling easier if you can obtain them or if you can afford them. Much work will be required nonetheless. Potential ticket buyers must somehow find out that a performance is going to take place, and once they find out, they must be convinced that they should attend. Visibility is only part of the battle; actually selling the tickets will be the result of personal solicitations, mailings, telephone campaigns, and more.

It will be important to have enough staff or volunteers at your disposal, to mobilize them effectively, to organize their activities in the proper sequence, and to have the patience and presence of mind to make sure that every planned maneuver goes off like clockwork. In the following pages, some of the proven methods for getting people to attend events will be described. Carried out faithfully, these methods may well lead to the happiest of outcomes—people beating down your door trying to gain entrance.[4]

RULE 16

You have to MAKE it happen.

Always assume that no one will come unless you have done everything humanly possible to convince them to come.

A full-scale audience development campaign begins with good planning, which should begin at the same time that you start thinking about what you are going to present. As you develop the schedule of events, you must also sketch out the timing of your promotional and ticket-selling activity. Several categories of activities must be considered:

DIRECT MAIL. Much promotion and ticket selling are done through the mail. You must think about the design and production of the brochure or other direct-mail devices that will provide information to ticket buyers and others. You must assemble and coordinate the various mailing lists you want to use. You must lay out a mailing schedule. You must design a system that will track the results so you can continually improve your direct-mail efforts from year to year.

FREE OR LOW-COST PUBLICITY. The most creative presenters find a variety of free or very low-cost ways to promote their events. They print their schedules in church bulletins or on book markers which can be given out at stores; they do displays (with relevant recordings) in record-store windows; they make up simple flyers which can be stuffed in with utility bills and bank statements; they print bureau cards that are included in hotel guest rooms and at the desk in the lobby; and they get supermarkets to do imprints on their paper bags.

One of the most effective forms of free publicity is word of mouth. One presenter put it this way:

> All the highfalutin market research techniques, algorithmic factor-weighting formulas, psychographic segmentation methodologies, and high-priced computer applications in the world will never equal the relationship opportunities, person-to-person communications, and sense of community that exist naturally in a grass-roots community—be it small town, urban neighborhood, or rural valley. There's no marketing or advertising technique anywhere that can build audiences and enlist support for the arts like an enthusiastic community member talking up last night's performance over a drug store counter. . . . Marketing at the grass-roots level is about people talking to one another, building community together, sharing and creating vision together, and reaping their reward together.[5]

PAID ADVERTISING. Paid advertising has increasingly become part of the budgets of even small presenting organizations. Print advertising in newspapers and magazines is most common, though radio and television advertising is becoming a more important part of the mix.

RULE 17

Check the COMPETITION.

Your first move should be to clear the dates of your events so that they do not conflict with other presentations, church choir rehearsals, civic club meetings, or other forms of nightly entertainment.

It is truly astounding how many activities take place in cities and towns. For the manager of a performing arts presenting organization, this fact is often learned the hard way. No sooner are the dates for performances selected and announced than potential ticket buyers start explaining why they will not be able to be there. "I must go to recorder group" —". . . to my Tuesday night choir rehearsal (I've never missed it in seventeen years)" — ". . . to the Altrusa Club meeting (didn't you know that we always meet on the first Tuesday of the month?)" — ". . . to the high school basketball play-off" —and so it goes. Occasionally, of course, these explanations are polite excuses by people who never intended to come to your events anyway, but often they are legitimate.

Check the COMPETITION.

In the long term, the best way to make sure that your events do not conflict with those of other organizations is to become part of various community networks of arts, entertainment, and service organizations. By talking with colleagues and sharing plans, you can often cooperate on scheduling and avoid conflicts before they occur. A bonus is that cooperative ventures, such as extended residencies, co-sponsorships, or joint promotional campaigns, sometimes grow out of such informal or formal associations. One group, located in a community of fewer than 10,000 people, cooperates on a joint summer calendar of events which promotes the area to tourists who travel the state. If such groups do not exist in your community, take the initiative to form one. Often a series of phone calls and a few meetings can develop a cooperative spirit.

Clearing dates is not easy. In fact, there will always be conflicts, and some must be taken more seriously than others. It is a good idea to consider conflicts with national and religious holidays or events, such as election day or Super Bowl Sunday. The programming calendar produced annually by the Association of Performing Arts Presenters includes most of the holidays and events to be considered. It is also important to consider local customs and activities. If most of the music lovers in town belong to the church choir, then it is foolhardy to schedule a concert on rehearsal night. Members of your committee should discuss dates with various people in town who are up-to-date on local activities. Be sure to check with the chamber of commerce and with churches, schools, and other nonprofit organizations to find out what events are already planned for the coming season. Sometimes, a local arts agency or other organization may maintain a calendar of arts events, and it is important to check these sources carefully.

Once you have chosen dates and time slots, you should get the word out to other groups before they schedule competing events for the same times. First, it is important to place your dates on community-wide calendars such as those already described. A more generalized strategy for ensuring that other events will not be planned for the nights you desire for your performances is to work toward a consistent schedule that becomes known around town. If you have one event a month, try to have it fall on the same day (the second Tuesday of every month, for example). If you have an event every week, you might try to make it fall on the same day and have it begin at the same time each week.

Once other organizations begin to realize your consistency in scheduling, they will try to avoid the dates you generally use. Just as you know that Rotary meets every Thursday at 1:00, so the Rotarians will come to know that Tuesday night is performance night in town. If possible, your promotional materials should state this plainly: "Molto Music Presents Eight Tuesday Evenings of Concerts." If you make the timing of your events consistent, your audience will habitually reserve your time slot as they plan their activities for the week or month.

However, many communities simply cannot dictate the day when an artist or performing group will come to town. Touring schedules and itineraries often require that a presenter accept a certain date or pass up the opportunity of presenting a particular performer or performing group. Although scheduling consistency is desirable, programming excellence is more critical. Presenters need to maintain some flexibility even while attempting consistency.

RULE 18

Use publicity materials that look PROFESSIONAL.

Promotional materials that look cheap have an odd effect on their viewers. Instead of the intended effect (My, how wise of the organization to put its money into programming rather than advertising), a frequent thought is: Ah, cheap materials, amateurish organization. They probably present second-rate stuff.

High-quality promotional materials need not be excessively expensive, particularly if a local artist can be convinced to do some designing in exchange for a couple of subscription tickets. One successful concert organization had a beautiful silk screen designed for its program covers about nine seasons ago. It is still being used, printed by volunteers who also print the same design onto posters. A local printer takes the programs and posters after the design has been run off in bright colors; he then prints the necessary black type at a nominal charge.

Many people think that hiring a designer is prohibitively expensive. Two things must be kept in mind, however. First, the cost of the designer is often a one-time expense. If you like what he or she has done for your organization, it can usually be used season after season with only minor changes. Second, though you will have to pay designers for their services, they can often find ways to save you money—their knowledge of materials and printers may make up for a portion of their fee.

Where should your organization begin when the time comes to have promotional materials designed? First, someone should be hired to design an identifying logo or line drawing that can be easily adapted for use on stationery, programs, posters, and flyers. The design should be simple without excessive detail. The finished design should show up well on various background colors.

Use publicity materials that look PROFESSIONAL.

THE
FEDERZEICHNUNGEN
TRITET
"See them to believe them." The Daily Moon
"A... routine you'll never forget."... anonymous
"I saw them perform in Madrid and I haven't recovered yet." J. Shedd, critic, Evening Sun

Most successful organizations print stationery, brochures, and posters. For would-be ticket buyers, a letter describing your plans is desirable but not enough. You will need to print up an attractive brochure with an order blank. The brochure should give the details of each event—date, time, performers, program—and should have some pertinent biographical material on the performers. Some successful organizations, for example, send a flyer that, when unfolded, lists all season events with the contents of each program on one side of the sheet. Subscribers can attach this sheet to a bulletin board as a reminder, and the presenting organization can use extra flyers in other sorts of promotional activities.

Some presenters find posters effective, especially in locales with a lot of foot traffic. Posters also appear to be effective with younger audiences, such as college students. Attractive posters can be designed inexpensively as throwaways or can be carefully and handsomely designed as commemorative pieces suitable for framing and selling as a fund-raising device. If you are planning to have a poster for advertising purposes, it must be printed on heavy paper or cardboard in a standard size large enough to be read at a distance. Simple posters are most effective. Keep the amount of type to a minimum and combine it with some eye-catching visual material printed in a color that is unlikely to fade excessively when exposed to continual sunlight. For some of your events, the performing group may provide you with preprinted posters and flyers as part of its press kit. A space will be provided where your printer can insert the date, time, and place of the performance. A less expensive alternative is to print "crack-and-peel" labels which can be affixed to the poster.

Two or more colors on a brochure and poster are always desirable. Often one of the colors will be black or something dark for the type, so the designer actually has only a single color to play with for visual effect. If you cannot afford more than one color, consider printing the type on colored stock. This often looks more attractive than black on white, but you must choose a background color that allows sufficient contrast for the printed type. Stay away from exotic typefaces, even if a particular one captures your fancy as you are looking through a type specimen catalogue. These so-called display types are more difficult to read. It is also generally undesirable to use several typefaces because doing so also cuts down on readability and visual consistency.

When deciding on the quantity of printed material you will need, remember that most of the cost goes into design, setup, and press time. The extra copies you order will be only as expensive as the paper or card stock they are printed on. For example, the difference in cost between 2,000 and 3,000 brochures may only be 10 percent of the total original estimate. If you have too many items printed up, there is no harm done and little financial loss. But if you underestimate and must do a second press run, your costs will be high.

Many organizations at some point face the question of whether it is necessary to put money into designing and printing posters and other promotional displays at all. Why not do everything by hand? There are often more than enough volunteers around to do posters in paint, crayon, or magic marker.

If you are considering this option, there is one very simple rule: don't! Posters that are done by hand automatically reflect a lack of professionalism on the part of the presenting organization. The following anecdote is a case in point:

> I once attended a performance as an evaluator for a funding agency. Everything about the event was handled in a professional manner; the performance was superb; the hall was filled. After the concert, I was invited to a reception with other arts administrators representing various organizations in that state. As I walked in, I heard the following comment by one of the guests to the executive director: "All these years, I never realized what marvelous stuff you do here. I did see your posters, of course, but because they were hand done and were not very professional, I just assumed that I wasn't missing much."

The key phrase in the remark quoted above is "not very professional." It is not that the speaker objected to things made by hand—he himself was wearing a beautiful hand-made shirt. It is simply that top-flight organizations do not allow their promotional materials to be produced in this fashion.

Once your promotional materials are ready, make a concerted effort to distribute them widely. Do not limit yourself to local outlets. Find out how far people in your area are likely to drive to attend events. Then consult a map and get members of the organization to help you take posters and brochures to every conceivable kind of location within a reasonable distance. Be sure that colleges and universities in your area have received your materials. Distribute to chambers of commerce, tourist information centers, motels, and restaurants. In general, when in doubt, go ahead and distribute your promotional information to a particular site. At the worst, your materials will be thrown away. At best, they will attract new customers.

Develop EXCITING promotional material.

RULE 19

Develop EXCITING promotional material.

Most presenters use a brochure as the anchor piece for their promotional campaigns. It is the item that carries the themes, messages, and images of the offerings and that may entice potential attenders either via direct mail or other distribution outlets. Brochures may be elaborate and expensive, but the ultimate test of a brochure, like all promotional material, is whether it invites perusal. Simply including lots of information does not necessarily mean that people will read it. Indeed, your publicity should include only the most interesting and essential information presented in a lively and engaging way.

To ensure that your publicity is effective, make sure you get promotional materials from the performers well before you think you may need them. If a group is to perform in the spring, but your first promotional pieces must come out in the fall, make sure the group is aware that you need their materials at the beginning of the summer. (If they are sending you items like posters to promote the performance itself, these should also be sent well before they will be needed.) The very least you should expect to receive are high-quality photographs and some written material including biographical data and excerpts from reviews. Often the group will have its own press kit, which will include everything you need for the brochure as well as press releases, ad slicks, and occasionally slides or a video. Even when this is the case, the quantity and timing of the receipt of these materials are subject to negotiation and should be included in your contract with the artist. It is wise to keep in touch with artists or their agents to remind them that you are expecting the materials.

Do not assume that the written material that will be sent to you will be usable in the form in which you receive it. Many fine performing groups send poorly written press releases or, worse yet, a set of biographies. You, or someone from your organization, may have to rework this material into a form sufficiently engaging and interesting, whether it is used in the promotional brochure or in a press release.

Finding people who can write effective promotional copy should be a top priority task for your organization. Quite simply, lively prose helps to sell tickets. The person selected to write should be familiar with the kind of information that people expect to see in descriptions of performing groups. The copy should be drawn from biographical information, reviews, listings of places where the group was well received, information on the selection of works to be performed, and

Start your subscription campaign EARLY.

so forth. The writing itself should be clear and enthusiastic, but always concise. As one newspaper person humorously put it, "short, direct sentences with words of one syllable or less."

In writing for the press or for your organization's promotional use, you must always think in terms of selling a product rather than merely announcing an event. To do so, appeal to a kind of objective index of quality so commonly used by advertisers. For most people, good reviews in major newspapers serve this function; to a lesser degree, a tour itinerary to foreign cities or major cities in the United States indicates that the performing group is probably of high caliber; finally, a testimonial from a celebrity—a famous performer in the same field or someone well known in the community—is helpful in establishing the credibility of the performing group.

If you do not find the kinds of things you want when you receive the group's promotional materials, call the agent and see whether you can get what you think you need. Sometimes performers have it but will not send it unless asked—keep in mind that their publicity materials cost money to produce and to ship. Some performers include material about their teachers or the institutions where members of the group studied. Although this information may be impressive to fellow performers, it generally means nothing to most readers—readers who will come to the performance only if they spot something that interests them.

RULE 20

Start your subscription campaign EARLY.

A ticket to a series of events is called a subscription. Selling subscriptions can be an extremely effective way to sell tickets. If five events are planned, selling a single subscription is equivalent to selling five individual tickets, except that it involves only a fraction of the work. A great advantage of subscription selling is that it brings in large amounts of cash early in the season when money may be desperately needed. In addition, successful subscription selling is usually an indication that there will be a good box office on performance night.

Today, subscription selling is on the decline in some areas. Increasingly, potential ticket buyers are busy people with unpredictable schedules, so they are often less willing to commit to a set number of events on specific dates over an extended period of time. Some presenters have modified their subscription offerings either by allowing greater flexibility in program choice, liberal exchange policies, or shorter series (or mini-series options) with fewer events. Some have even chosen to put all their efforts into selling single tickets and have abandoned the subscription approach altogether.

Deciding whether to introduce or to continue a subscription campaign is like any other kind of cost-benefit analysis. You must first figure out the amount of time and money that will have to be expended and then determine how many subscriptions it will take to justify this outlay. This is why it is so important even for experienced presenters to track the results of their efforts, modifying campaigns to increase the ratio of income to cost.

Should you decide to proceed with a subscription campaign, it is important to decide what enticements you will offer to those who commit to purchasing tickets for a number of events. Some organizations give large discounts. However, it is important to remember that, for the more affluent who will be the target of these appeals, saving money may be a less important motivator than other enticements—first choice of seat location, receptions with artists, or parking benefits. It is generally advantageous to offer flexibility to subscribers and liberal exchange policies, but it is not a good idea to offer refunds when they cannot use tickets for a particular event. Instead, subscribers should be encouraged to call in unused tickets in advance; you can promise them a receipt for a tax-deductible contribution for the value of the tickets turned in.

Subscription selling should begin early—not less than two months before the first scheduled performance and often considerably earlier. There is no reliable rule of thumb to determine whether your subscription campaign is going well or is lagging. In certain communities and for certain audiences, a great number of subscriptions will be sold, accounting for perhaps 75 percent of the seats in the house. In other cases, most tickets will be sold as singles during the week of the performance or at the door on performance night. One successful presenting organization whose hall has a 400-seat capacity has found that if the auditorium is 25 percent sold with subscriptions one week before the first concert of the season, most of the series events will be sold out. Although this formula is unique to this organization, it is useful for others also to analyze subscription sales relative to total ticket sales in order to project a realistic goal for the ticket committee at the beginning of each season.

Most subscription campaigns are conducted by mail, so an accurate, up-to-date mailing list is essential. If you are starting a mailing list for the first time, you should borrow or purchase local lists from organizations that cater to the kinds of people who are likely to come to your events. Do not limit yourself to arts organizations, though these are good bets. Consider lists from churches, clubs, libraries, the chamber of commerce, even retail outlets that do business by mail or local subscription lists for magazines. Once you have a basic list, continue to add names to it. Every time a ticket is sold, attempt to capture the name and address of the ticket buyer. Write down the names and addresses of people when you find them on checks and place mailing list cards in your programs and at strategic locations during performances. The cards should say that by filling them out, individuals will get advance notice of events or, if you publish one, a free newsletter.

Whether you are attempting to attract subscribers or merely trying to sell renewals, direct solicitation by phone is always effective. The person being solicited will usually find it difficult to say no or to postpone a decision when a friend or volunteer is waiting on the other end of the line. The telephone is especially effective in getting lapsed subscribers back into the fold. At the very least, a phone call may garner important information about why an individual has not subscribed. For example, one organization saw itself losing its older subscribers and found that most were unwilling to go out at night. A mini-series of matinees not only got these people to resubscribe but attracted a whole new constituency that had not attended performances in the past.

In planning a telephone campaign, staff or volunteers can divide up the list of potential buyers, with each person taking responsibility for phoning several names on the list. It is always useful to script the volunteers so they do not find themselves tongue-tied. But they should feel comfortable about departing from the script at any time. If your potential list of subscribers or ticket buyers is large, you can resort to paid telemarketing campaigns. However, most smaller organizations find that would-be ticket buyers are much more responsive to calls from volunteers or regular staff.

Once you have a subscriber base, plans need to be made each year for the annual renewal campaign. Subscribers should be given advance notice of the season, first opportunity to purchase tickets, first choice of seat location, and various other benefits. Placing a time limit on these benefits is often a great motivator in securing subscribers' renewed commitment.

Work CLOSELY with newspapers.

RULE 21

Work CLOSELY with newspapers.

Work with local, regional, and statewide newspapers. A loyal newspaper can be a promotional person's best friend.

Despite the growing importance of radio and television in getting your message to potential ticket buyers, newspapers still provide the most economical method of doing so. By printing press releases and calendar listings and by agreeing to do occasional feature stories, newspapers provide free advertising which reaches a great number of people. In addition, most presenters find it advisable to purchase advertising space as well.

The logical time to advertise is during the campaign to sell subscriptions (before the season begins) and during the weeks before each individual event. If your first event is to take place on October 1, you may well want to run a large ad in the middle of September listing the dates, performers, and programs for each event and including a cut-out coupon that can be sent in as a ticket order form. You can also run a small ad on the day before or the day of each event, or both, reminding people where tickets may be purchased. If you are located near a college or university, consider advertising in the campus paper; the rates are usually a bargain.

Some newspapers, especially those in smaller communities, may help you design your ads. If you plan to take advantage of this service, provide the newspaper with a basic design and the exact typed information to be included. For visual variety, you can use your organization's logo—excellent for establishing an identity—or a photograph of the performing group. Sometimes the performing group you are hiring will supply ad slicks, and the newspaper can then add local information about the time and place of the event.

In most cases, presenters have found that it pays to use the services of a professional designer, particularly if a specific format can be designed once and reused frequently. Whether or not you do, you should be careful not to fill the ad with a lot of prose. Rather, you should include eye-catching visuals and a minimum of type. Be sure to incorporate large, bold type either to identify your organization and the performing group or to point out something special about the event (for example, "A Few Tickets Still Available"; "Special Mime Show Tonight"; "Reduced Prices for Students and Senior Citizens").

An excellent form of free advertising is the press release, which can be sent, along with photographs, to any newspapers that conceivably might run it (for a sample press release, see appendix C). Find out which editor or department should receive your release and try to develop a personal relationship with the person who regularly handles your copy. The release should be typed on plain white paper or the organization's stationery. It should be double- or triple-spaced with ample margins. At the top left, type the name, address, and phone number of your organization plus the name of a contact person. On the top right, type the date on which you want the story run, for example, "FOR IMMEDIATE RELEASE: January 15, 1992"). You may want to suggest a headline (if so, keep it short), or you may leave the headline blank. The release should run about 350 words or less. If it runs more than a page, type the word "MORE" at the bottom of the first sheet and type a string of *X*'s at the end of the article. The photo that you send along with the story should include a short identifying caption on the back. Send only photographs with good contrast. Do not send ones that are too dark or diffuse.

A newspaper is in the business of printing news; hence, the press release must read as a news story. The first paragraph should begin with the vital statistics on the event (day, time, location, performing group, presenting organization, place where tickets can be bought, and so forth). The next paragraph should contain the most exciting material about the event or the group being presented. Sentences, particularly in the beginning, should be short; the content, clear. The philosophy behind these rules is simple. Most readers will scan the article casually, only reading the first couple of paragraphs. In addition, there is no guarantee that the newspaper will use your release in its entirety. More than likely the story will be cut to fit into a certain space. As a general rule, cuts are made from the bottom up. The newspaper staff will usually not take the time to read over the cut article to see if it still makes sense. As a result, the material near the end of your release should be nonessential information conveniently packaged in self-sufficient paragraphs.

In attempting to come up with interesting copy for newspapers, do not despair if you cannot get interesting materials from the performers. You do not have to write about them. There are always other newsworthy alternatives. After announcing an upcoming event, structure your story around some other news: the recent grant from the state arts council, the after-concert reception, the new piano your organization just purchased. The essential information about the performance will still be contained in the first paragraph and those who read on will be treated to an interesting story.

At the same time that someone is writing press releases, the organization should be inviting newspaper writers as well as other media people to each event. Set aside press tickets and encourage regular reviews. Your audiences will like to read about events they have attended, and the reviews also serve as advertising for those who did not attend. Newspaper and magazine staff writers can also write feature stories. To persuade a newspaper to run a feature, you may want to promise the writer "an exclusive"—essentially a promise that you will not give the same story to someone else working for a competing publication. Feature stories, which are generally handled carefully by the newspaper writers, are often run with several pictures and printed in a more prominent location than a press release sent by your organization.

Features tend to be in-depth stories of an organization and its activities. They are less oriented toward announcing upcoming events—though they do contain such news—and more toward a study of the individuals connected with the organization, their motivations, goals, frustrations, hopes. Such stories not only represent a valuable form of exposure at the time they appear but become part of the promotional package that the organization presents to its contributors, funding agencies, and other supporters. There is a good deal of work associated with feature stories—interesting the newspaper staff, arranging for interviews and photography sessions—but the effort is usually well worthwhile.

In addition to a feature story, press releases, and paid advertisements, your organization should make use of one more promotional service offered by some newspapers and magazines—the community calendar. Calendars are listings of events taking place during a particular week or month. If you send a list of your programs to the proper person or department at the newspaper offices, there is a good chance that each will be listed at the appropriate time. Most calendars have deadlines that are usually well ahead of the date the listing will run. The larger the publication, the earlier the deadline. For example, a small community-based organization in New England may be able to get into the summer calendar listings in the *New York Times,* but only if it gets its material in before the March deadline. The time differential between deadline and listing is not as extreme for smaller newspapers, but it is usually significant and extensions are almost never granted. Airline and regional magazines regularly run calendars that are consulted by both local residents and visitors and should also be considered.

Use the RADIO and TV, too.

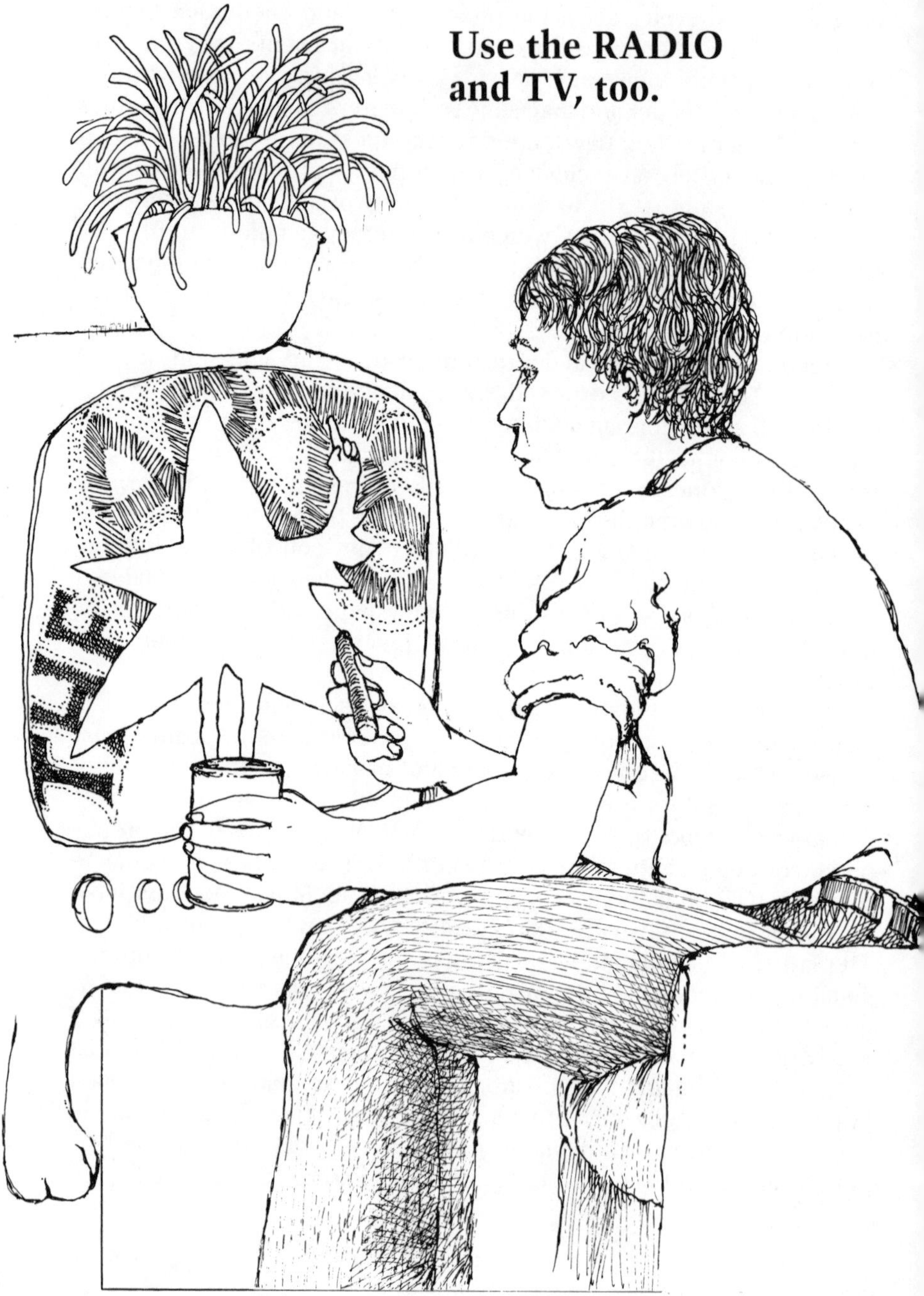

RULE 22

Use the RADIO and TV, too.

Use radio and TV to promote your organization's activities. If you cannot afford to advertise, consider becoming a "star for a day."

Like newspapers, radio and television offer several options to organizations wishing to promote their activities. These include public service announcements, advertising, and the interview/talk show. In thinking about radio possibilities, you should consider both commercial and public stations and use both AM and FM. Television outlets include public and commercial network stations as well as the ever-growing number of cable stations across the country. In some markets, foreign-language radio and television stations should be seriously considered as a way to reach targeted audiences, particularly for events that may have special appeal.

A public-service announcement is the equivalent of a free ad. Public-service announcements can range from a typed message for a radio announcer to read on air to a fully produced video for television. Either will fit into the format of a 10-, 20-, or 30-second "spot," but those that are more interesting and more professionally produced have a better chance of being aired. Sometimes performing groups can provide an audio or videotape that allows the local presenter to add local information as a voice-over or at the end of the spot. At other times a local advertising firm, sound engineer, or video producer might donate services to produce an interesting and engaging spot. One small community presenter has a beautifully produced 20-second video that it uses over and over again with changing audio to promote whatever event is current.

Many radio and television stations, like newspapers, run a local calendar. In larger markets, there may be an "arts calendar," and it is a must to get your events promoted as part of this listing. In other cases, the calendar is more generic and the free service is used by many kinds of community organizations, such as church groups, service clubs, the YMCA, and the Boy Scouts. Because this generic community calendar is rarely run during prime time and because it does not emphasize arts and entertainment, it is rarely heard by many of the people you would like to reach. Nevertheless, it is an opportunity for exposure which should not be ignored. Call the station and find out when and where your listing should be sent. The deadline is rarely more than a week ahead of the broadcast day, and often the listing can be received as little as a day ahead.

Another form of free advertising is the radio or television interview. Because hosts and producers like to interview "personalities"—people who have done exotic and unusual things—you are more likely to obtain an invitation and have an interesting show if you can get one of the performers to do the show or go along with you. However, this is not always a prerequisite for getting on the air. It is a good idea to take along a typed set of suggested questions and some printed background material, because few hosts take a lot of time to prepare the show.

Radio and television advertising, which can be costly, often brings significant returns in ticket sales. A nonprofit organization will sometimes be able to negotiate a special advertising rate. For example, some stations will donate one advertisement for each one that the organization pays for. In some cases, radio stations will negotiate a lower rate if you can provide a giveaway (free tickets, tapes, compact discs) on the air. Ads (or spots) are priced on the basis of their length in seconds (for example, ten, fifteen, twenty, thirty, or sixty seconds) and the time at which they are aired (for radio, morning and evening drive time is the most expensive; for television, prime time is the most expensive). In general, several short spots are more desirable than one or two long ones if your main concern is to announce an upcoming event.

If you are writing the material for a radio ad, keep it simple. You might begin with the essential information (date, time, place of the event, and where tickets can be purchased), or you might begin with an enthusiastic statement about the performing group. Whichever format you choose, be sure to repeat the essential information at the end of the ad. Although the radio station will be happy to read the material you send them, produced ads—like the public-service announcements described earlier—will be more effective than those simply read by the radio announcer. Produced ads are a requirement for television.

Selecting the radio and television stations with which your organization should do business can be tricky and time-consuming. Much time and money can be wasted if you promote your events on stations whose listeners are unlikely to attend. In general, there is a high correlation between people who attend performing arts events and those who listen to public broadcasting, so this is an important place to begin. Though public stations do not carry advertising, they offer calendars, interviews, and giveaways. They also "sell" the equivalent of advertising through program sponsorship, and it is sometimes advantageous for larger presenters to consider this. At the very least, presenters should call the public radio and television stations that service their area and find out whether someone from the organization or a performer can be interviewed. In some cases, interviews can be done by phone.

In addition to public broadcasting, the possibilities are numerous. Your own local radio stations are always a possibility, but you must determine how many potential ticket buyers you will reach by using them. One way to do so is to consult what are called "Arbitron" listings, which can be found at radio stations or advertising agencies. These provide the profile and size of listenership of radio station audiences at various times of the day.

RULE 23

Make it EASY to get tickets.

In today's world, convenience is a byword of selling. People are used to picking up the phone and placing an order quickly, using a credit card. Walk-in sales are promoted by convenient hours and locations. For small presenting organizations, particularly those with few if any staff members, making tickets available at a box office for extended hours each day is simply impossible. Therefore, it is important to investigate other options.

In some cases, presenters may get ticket-selling services for free from a local bookstore, record store, or gift shop. Many of these in-town shops are willing to sell the tickets in exchange for the free publicity they receive. The reasoning goes something like this: people who have the money to buy tickets for a performing arts event are potential customers for other things as well. Thus, if tickets are sold at the local bookstore, prospective book customers can be lured into the store when they come to purchase their tickets. In this manner, most presenting organizations can find other business concerns that are willing to handle the pre-performance sale of tickets. In many cases, the presenter will still handle phone orders and must carefully monitor the reserved tickets that are available at its ticket-selling locations.

Most presenters should be able to offer the convenience of credit card sales by phone. Making an arrangement with a local bank generally is simple and allows the organization to accept Mastercard and VISA at a minimum. If the phone cannot be answered by someone at all hours, an answering machine can tell the caller what hours someone will be available or can suggest that he or she leave a name and telephone number. Presenters should always list themselves in the telephone directory yellow pages—under ticket agencies, theaters, or other relevant categories.

Make it EASY to get tickets.

There are other box office services that presenters can use. Some local arts agencies run communitywide box offices. Commercial computerized ticketing services are available on a fee basis. Colleges and universities often have a centralized ticket-selling service. Whatever systems are chosen, they should meet the needs of your potential ticket buyers. You must adapt to their habits and service them rather than the other way around.

It is important to make it easy for people to buy tickets, and it is equally important to demand fair market value. Beware of pricing your tickets too inexpensively. To potential ticket buyers, the price of the ticket is a reflection of what you think the evening's entertainment is worth.

Reflect for a moment on your own thoughts as you look through a price list of performing groups. You probably glance at the name of each group, scan the descriptions, and look closely at the prices. If your eye catches a price that seems high, your first reaction may be: That group is too expensive for us; I won't bother to read about them. Or you may think: Hmm, these people are pretty expensive. They must be good. Let's see what they have done.

If you are like most people, the second reaction describes what is probably going through your mind. This is the way the psychology of pricing in the performing arts seems to work. If tickets are free or very inexpensive, part of the potential audience may stay home, convinced that the offerings are second rate. Conversely, if the tickets are moderately expensive, people may assume that your organization is offering high-quality events. Many organizations believe that the way to increase the size of the audience is to lower ticket prices. Time and time again, this turns out not to be true. In fact, it often works the other way: when ticket prices go up, so does the demand for tickets.

The danger, of course, is that only the well-to-do will attend your events if ticket prices are too high. But ask yourself this question: is the reason that less affluent people are not attending because of ticket prices? Many of these nonattenders who are not buying your tickets are regular moviegoers and do not balk at paying at a movie theater just as much or more than you are charging. Perhaps, therefore, it is not price that is keeping them away; it is lack of interest in what you are presenting. Everyone agrees that the broadest possible public should become motivated to attend performing arts events. Everyone agrees that your organization should make a concerted effort to reach as many people as possible. Do not assume, however, that you will be successful in the effort simply by lowering your ticket prices.

There is no question that some quite genuinely cannot afford to purchase expensive tickets to a performing arts event. These people

Make the night of the performance something SPECIAL.

usually fall into predictable groups: students, senior citizens, families with several children, and so forth. For each of these target populations, the organization can offer less expensive tickets. Students with a proper I.D. traditionally receive discounts, and the trend is toward offering the same rate to people over the age of sixty-five. For families, a special group rate can be offered. If a parent buys a ticket at the full price, each child might be admitted for a token fee or at no cost. Remember that there are always ways to make less expensive tickets available without sacrificing income from those who can afford to buy the full-priced tickets.

RULE 24

Make the night of the performance something SPECIAL.

Always capitalize on the fact that attendance at your performances gives people the opportunity to have a night out.

Why do people attend performing arts events? Is it simply because they enjoy music, dance, theater? Of course not. People like to go out and do something special. It can be fun and relaxing, a chance to see one's friends, an opportunity to be seen in good company. Indeed, performing arts events are social events, and the most successful presenters capitalize on this fact in their attempts to fill the auditorium.

One of the most obvious ways to take advantage of the social aspect of performing arts events is to attempt to sell tickets to groups of people who ordinarily do things together. Occasionally special inducements can be offered when a block sale is negotiated. Large groups, such as the local garden club, church group, dance school, or music conservatory, may be convinced to purchase tickets *en bloc* if they are offered a discount.

Presenting organizations can sometimes increase the size of the audience through specific social activities. One of the most popular is the pre-performance party. Several members of the board or other friends of the organization may give cocktail or dinner parties immediately preceding the performance. They may invite some of the regular subscribers, but they should also include a number of people who would not normally attend. Most of the guests will probably go from the party to the performance.

BUILD your audience over time.

More elaborate devices exist for making the evening's entertainment something special. Occasionally one of the restaurants in town may be willing to promote a "Concert Dinner" for people holding tickets to the performance. On the evening of the concert, ticket holders are offered a different menu (at a special price) if they come between 5:30 and 6:30 p.m. Alternatively, a restaurant or pub might consent to a similar arrangement for food or drink after the event.

After the performance it is common to give a reception for the artists. Because people like to meet performers, the reception may be planned carefully as a way to sell more subscriptions or tickets. Some organizations use the artist-reception as one of the incentives for subscribers (one organization calls them "Subscriber Parties"). In other cases, the entire audience is invited to an informal "Meet the Artists" reception in the auditorium immediately following the performance. Publicity materials may stress that anyone who buys a ticket is welcome to attend.

Many presenters have a tendency to become so involved in artistic and administrative details that they forget the social aspect of attendance at performances. For these presenters, it is helpful to have a few board members who can suggest how to make the best use of social opportunities in promoting the events. Underestimating the importance of this effort can be costly.

RULE 25

BUILD your audience over time.

Building audiences is a challenge for most presenters. There is usually a core group who will attend many of the events; but there are others in the community who are simply uninterested. It is easy to blame this on high ticket prices, bad publicity, or the inconvenience of ticket outlets. Yet these are usually a small part of the problem.

Many people simply do not feel comfortable going into a fancy auditorium, particularly when they believe that what will be presented will be over their heads, boring, or worse. Although there are no easy solutions, certain things can be done, over time, that seem to encourage people to sample events for the first time.

First, begin to consider performing spaces other than concert halls or theaters. As has already been discussed in connection with residencies, it may be possible to have a performing group present work in schools, local libraries, civic clubs, banks, offices, and stores. Remember that part of the problem is exposure. To many in your community, your organization may appear elitist, serving esoteric entertainment to the chosen few. You can begin to break down this image by bringing the performing groups to the community. At each informal event, announce any upcoming performances. People may follow up their initial interest by attending these performances, and they will certainly tell their friends about what they have seen and heard.

Second, look carefully at your program offerings. Are they too limited in their appeal? Do they reflect only one art form or cultural tradition? If so, perhaps you might consider broadening your programming philosophy to encompass more of your community and their interests. Find out what specific groups in your community—from among those who are not now attenders—might wish to see or hear. Solicit their opinions and explore a variety of programming options. Although part of your mission should be to guide people to new experiences in the arts, you should also be open-minded about being guided by others.

Third, if you want to build a new audience, you must make people feel a part of your organization. Start by inviting a neighbor or acquaintance to a performance as your guest and encouraging or requiring board members to do the same. Organize a group to go to dinner before the performance or to go out afterward. Introduce first-time attenders to the performers. Eventually, some of these people may become enthusiastic supporters and end up buying tickets on their own. If they continue to be enthusiastic, follow up with a request for some volunteer help. Ask if they would be interested in bringing friends to the next event. From these first tentative associations, new members of your audience can be developed.

Once a number of new people have become associated with the organization in this fashion, one or two should be invited to serve on the board. You may be surprised just how helpful they can be in building the size and variety of your audience. Often these new board members can reach out to segments of the community that you have never reached before. It is important to remember, however, that it takes a long time to change attendance patterns. Building a new and bigger audience is hard work—work that demands your attention and effort. Audience building, after all, is one form of survival insurance.

Conclusion

If this chapter has had one theme it is that filling an auditorium is not simply a matter of hiring big-name talent, being blessed with an arts-conscious community, or being lucky. All of these things help, of course, but what really counts is your willingness and the willingness of others in your community to put in many hours of hard work. If people are unwilling to put in these hours, you might just as well close up shop, for in the long run you cannot survive. On the other hand, if you can garner the work force, you have a good chance of developing a loyal and committed audience.

Don't FANTASIZE!

4

Fund Raising

RULE 26

Don't FANTASIZE.

Fund raising is hard work, expensive, and time-consuming. The initial task must be to develop a credible argument for support.

Most fund raisers I have talked to admit that they occasionally fantasize about collecting money from fabulously rich people. One fantasy, which seems almost universal, centers on a benevolent patron who offers to underwrite an organization's activities and cover all deficits, no strings attached. We may smile as we remind ourselves that twentieth-century Medicis are few and far between, but it is remarkable how many of us indulge in some variation of this fantasy without really being aware of it. Many small organizations, for example, spend hours, days, and weeks searching for major backers, pursuing such large funding sources as wealthy individuals, foundations, or the

National Endowment for the Arts. There is nothing wrong in developing fund-raising strategies for the "big angels." But the bread-and-butter support of small and successful community-based presenting organizations comes from a broad range of contributors, most of them modest donors who, collectively, give substantial sums of money. For these organizations, most donations come from local sources—from individuals, small businesses, municipal agencies.

These donors are valuable for several reasons. First, they often give money year after year, and once they are properly cultivated it is not a huge task to convince them to continue giving. Second, the dollars they give are, for the most part, unrestricted—that is, they do not have to be used for a specific project or program but can be used for basic administrative costs, rent, and other expenses for which substantial outside grants are rarely available. Finally, successful cultivation of these local donors leads to larger contributions from outside the community. Generally, unless an organization can show broad-based local support, major funding sources are uninterested in contributing to the cause.

One of the most important things to keep in mind, whether pursuing the large donor or the small contributor, is that your organization must first formulate a convincing case for support. Determining your "fundraisability" is a primary and ongoing task. You must develop a perspective toward your organization which allows you to pinpoint the specific activities most likely to have the greatest appeal to contributors. Do not ask people to cover a deficit. Rather, ask them to support an organization that provides arts programs for young people, that attracts visitors and adds to the economic vitality of the community, or that is involved in community ventures like arts festivals or downtown revitalization projects. If you are about to embark on a restoration project for your arts facility or if you are thinking of setting up a subsidized ticket program for senior citizens, let potential contributors know about these developments.

A second thing to keep in mind is that your organization must allow plenty of lead time in planning the fund-raising effort. If you are planning a fund-raising event, you may need to start recruiting volunteers a year ahead of time. Applications to state and federal agencies have filing deadlines that may be sixteen to eighteen months ahead of the specified project date. Lead time is also needed in local fund raising. If individual and business contributors are to be listed in a program, for example, solicitations must be made well ahead of the printer's deadline date. The fund-raising committee of the board of trustees, along with the staff, should always be working a couple of years ahead in developing an overall strategy, goal, and timetable for fund-raising activities. Working ahead gives your organization the additional advantage of collecting money for upcoming events, rather than asking contributors to pick up the deficit for the season already completed.

A third consideration in planning a fund-raising campaign is that it usually costs money to raise money. Whether the costs incurred are for printing and mailing letters, hiring additional staff, taking a potential contributor to lunch, or holding a fund-raising party, cash usually will have to be paid out before the returns come in. In the case of every expenditure, the organization will eventually have to resort to some form of cost-benefit analysis. What are the costs involved in bringing in a certain amount of cash? Should these costs be reduced? Can the take be increased?

The realistic fund raiser, then, is one who formulates a convincing case for support, focuses on developing a broad base of local contributors, allows plenty of lead time, and is conscious of the expenses entailed in a successful campaign for money. The purpose of this chapter is to provide some techniques that may prove helpful in the actual fund-raising efforts.

RULE 27

Make your fund-raising events LUCRATIVE.

Be sure your fund-raising events are as profitable as they are clever.

Have you ever heard about a fund-raising event that made you smile or burst out laughing? Innumerable gimmicks have been associated with such events. But the truth is, events are one of the most important fund-raising techniques that presenting organizations can employ in raising money from the local community. From bake sales to lavish media auctions, the fund-raising event is an excellent example of where cost-benefit analysis should be applied—yet often is not. Fund-raising events can make lots of money. They can attract contributors who might not otherwise consider donating to your organization. They can bring media exposure to the organization through a totally unrelated activity and spread the gospel of your good works throughout the community. Yet far too often, the fund-raising event represents an exhausting and time-consuming effort for its planners and executors—an effort out of proportion to the amount of net income realized. It is essential to remember that a successful fund-raising event does not necessarily prompt participant-contributors to spend a lot

Make your fund-raising events LUCRATIVE.

of money. The successful event is the one that leaves the organization with a sizable sum after all the bills are paid.

The devices that have been used successfully by presenting organizations in raising money through events include fashion shows, auctions, raffles, dinner dances, antique shows, cheese and wine parties, house or garden tours, and visits to artists' studios. Occasionally an organization will buy a block of tickets to a concert or play at a reduced rate and then sell seats to contributors at a higher price—for example, Boston Pops concerts are a favorite fund-raising event, and the orchestra regularly sells out its hall to other organizations doing ticket markups. More lavish projects include travel—a guided tour of European museums or musical cruises in the Mediterranean. In these cases, the contributor pays a lump sum that covers all expenses plus a contribution to the presenting organization. Less extravagant projects include benefit concerts, open rehearsals, and films. Often a special tribute may be paid to a loyal supporter (either living or dead) by associating his or her name with the event. This encourages friends and relatives to contribute generously and allows the organization a special opportunity to say thank you.

Most presenting organizations can and should do some sort of annual fund-raising event. One reason is that these events generally bring in much-needed unrestricted funds. Events are also useful ways to cultivate first-time donors, particularly local businesses that may be willing to make in-kind contributions (that is, contributions of goods or services rather than cash) for an event. Finally, events are one of the most effective ways of getting another contribution from your regular donors.

In trying to decide what sort of event to do, be sure to select something that your best prospects will think is fun. That will help ensure a good turnout. You should not proceed unless you have lots of volunteers and adequate time to plan and promote the event. Be sure to set a dollar goal early and stick to it—this will give volunteers something to aim for and in the end will be the best way to measure success. Finally, if you come up with an event format that people enjoy, stick with it for a few years. If people have had a good time, they can often be convinced to come again the following year and to bring their friends.

RULE ***28***

Make it EASY to contribute to your organization.

Most presenting organizations bring in many contributions from ticket buyers. The most successful ones do so by making it easy for

Make it EASY to contribute to your organization.

these people to contribute. They ask for money frequently and in a variety of ways—by making requests in conjunction with subscription sales, by holding special events (such as the ones just described), by sending out an annual appeal, by making targeted requests for particular needs, and so on. The fund raiser's general rule of thumb is: the more often you ask, the more you will get.

One of the oldest and most successful enticements for bringing in more money is to establish various contribution categories based on different dollar levels and gradually to get people to upgrade categories from year to year. To do so, the organization must decide if it wants to offer special benefits to encourage people to give at the higher levels. Sometimes these benefits are minimal (for example, special listings in the program); occasionally they are generous or lavish (for example, special seats in the auditorium, dinner with the performers, a framed poster signed by the performers, free admission to an open rehearsal). In general, the organization can get far more for its money—and provide more desirable benefits—by offering services and privileges rather than outright gifts of merchandise. Remember, it is always important to maximize income while minimizing the cost.

In some organizations, the stratified giving levels and benefits are directly linked to subscription selling, and people are encouraged to give at the same time they buy their tickets. Let us take a hypothetical example. An organization plans a series of five events. Subscriptions for the entire series sell for $60. However, subscribers are encouraged to give more than the $60 in the following special categories:

1. *Patron:* A patron buys a subscription for $250. This entitles him or her to a special listing in the program, first choice of seats, and an invitation to a special "contributors' reception" to which the performers will also be invited.

2. *Sponsor:* A sponsor buys a subscription for $150. This entitles him or her to a listing in the program and a choice of seats before the general mailing to ticket buyers.

3. *Contributor:* A contributor pays $100 for a subscription and is listed in the program.

In each of these categories, the purchasers can deduct for income tax purposes a certain sum of money as a contribution. The amount is calculated as the difference between the total payment and the value of the tickets (for instance, the patron's deduction would be $250 minus $60, or $190). In this case, or in the case of any contribution in which the donor receives something from the organization in return for the gift, it is the organization's responsibility to state the value of any premium or goods being provided. The best way to do so is to make

Concentrate your efforts on INDIVIDUAL contributors.

it clear in the original solicitation. It is also desirable for the donor to receive a receipt for the net contribution once it has been received.

Once you receive a contribution, it is essential to acknowledge it immediately—within a week to ten days. The more personal the acknowledgment, the better. Indeed, according to some donors, it is the warmth of thank-you notes that often makes them want to give again. Thank-you notes should be sure to mention the amounts of gifts so that donors have an official paper trail for the IRS in case they need to prove that the contribution was made. Some organizations include a tax receipt card as follows:

NAME OF ORGANIZATION

(Address)

gratefully acknowledges the contribution of

Name ______________________________

Address ______________________________

____

In the amount of ______________________

Date ______________________________

If these acknowledgments are printed on duplicate paper, the original can go to the donor and the copy can be put in the files. Some organizations like to have these cards sequentially numbered so that there is an additional way of verifying and checking records.

RULE 29

Concentrate your efforts on INDIVIDUAL contributors.

Two facts must be kept in mind when an organization decides where time, energy, and money should be expended for the purposes of fund raising. First, individuals contribute far more to charity than all other sources combined. Overall, more than 75 percent of private contributions to tax-exempt organizations are made by individuals. Second, individuals who contribute to nonprofit organizations are not only the rich. People with modest incomes also contribute generously. Do not make the mistake of dismissing individuals who are not obviously wealthy. Over time, many of these people may end up giving your organization a great deal of money.

It should be obvious, then, that the major emphasis of fund-raising efforts should be on individuals, that the prospect base should be broad, and that the number of ways to approach these individuals should be varied (not only do incomes vary but so do personal philosophies of giving).

Most presenting organizations should do an appeal once a year for unrestricted contributions. This appeal is separate from the fund-raising effort in conjunction with the subscription drive. The appeal is not directed at major givers, who would be solicited more personally and often in conjunction with a specific project. The central fund-raising device in an annual appeal is a letter (a sample fund-raising letter is included as Appendix D). Although the letter is often printed in quantity, the more personalized the approach to people, the greater likelihood of success. Thus, individual names and addresses on at least some of the letters are desirable, and this can be accomplished through a computerized mail merge from the organization's mailing list. Even preprinted "Dear Friend" letters can be personalized with a short handwritten cover note. For example, a volunteer might write the following on his or her personal stationery and enclose it with the preprinted letter as follows:

> Dear Jane and Bob,
>
> Your $50 gift meant a lot to us last year. With our expanded season, you might consider giving even more this year.
>
> My best wishes to you and yours.
>
> Sam

Alternatively, a handwritten "P.S." on the printed letter itself might read:

> P.S. As someone who loves the arts, I hope you will join us in supporting this great community asset.
>
> Mary Johnson (your neighbor)

The annual appeal letter itself should be printed on the organization's stationery. If the presenting organization has its own board, their names, and possibly the names of advisory committee members, should be listed in the left-hand margin. Potential contributors are often influenced by who is associated with the organization, particularly if these individuals are prominent in the community. The letter should be signed by the board president, the chairman of the fund-raising committee, or the artistic director—whichever name is thought to mean more to those receiving the letter. In some cases, two signatures will be appropriate.

The first sentence or paragraph of the letter will probably determine how much of it gets read. Begin with something clever, humorous, or otherwise engaging and make the appeal quickly and concisely. Even at its best, the entire letter will not be read carefully in most cases so do not go into endless detail. Limit yourself to three or four paragraphs—at most, a typed page. Do not beat around the bush. Do not pretend that it is not a fund-raising letter. If you do need to present some particular idea in detail, do so on a separate sheet of paper and refer to this material in the letter. A simple procedure is to refer to two or three accomplishments of the organization in the past year and to mention some specific projects to be undertaken in the upcoming season. You might end with a sentence like the following:

> We hope you will join Mayor Smith and the 207 other contributors who last year helped us to raise a record $15,035 for the ongoing work of our organization.

Along with the letter itself, include a return envelope in which the contributor can enclose a check. Also enclose a donor card on which the contributors can write their names and addresses, indicate the amount of their gifts, and let you know whether they want their names to be listed in programs and other material or kept anonymous. If you are offering the option of a credit-card payment, the necessary information and a place for a signature should also be included (see sample, p. 101).

Many annual appeals go out toward the end of the calendar year, which is when many people do most of their giving. If you plan to do your solicitation in the late fall, leave adequate time before the holidays to do a follow-up letter and phone call to those who have not responded. Persistence and repeated reminders are often successful.

RULE 30

Find benevolent ANGELS.

For contributors who might be willing and able to make sizable contributions (more than $500), personal solicitation is recommended. Here there are no hard-and-fast rules. Each potential contributor must

Find benevolent ANGELS.

Yes, I wish to contribute $ ____________

________ check enclosed

________ please bill my credit card as indicated below.

Name (as you wish it to appear) ______________________________

____

Address: ____

____

________ I wish my contribution to be anonymous

Credit card used: ____

Credit card #: ____

Expiration date: ____

Signature: ____

---

be considered as an individual, and the approach to each should be closely tied to what members know of his or her predilections and habits of giving.

In general, a board member who knows the individual should make an appointment for a personal visit. In certain cases, the artistic director or an articulate performer can sit in on the meeting to describe the program in some detail. The more specific the appeal, the greater the likelihood of success. It is often persuasive to use the following argument: "Five contributors are being asked to donate $500 [toward a specific project] and two have already said yes." This gives potential donors some assurance that they are joining in a worthy effort with others. For example, here is an actual case history:

> An organization finds that certain repairs have to be made on the interior of the building being used for performances. The building's owner says that he cannot afford the total cost of the improvements, but agrees to put up half of the $30,000 required. The organization has $5,000 put aside for

> emergency capital needs and thus needs a minimum of $10,000 more. Most institutional donors will not contribute funds for renovations. So the fund-raising committee decides to try to obtain a minimum of four $2,500 contributions (if it can find six, it will leave the $5,000 emergency fund intact). Two members of the committee who are board members agree to participate, thus providing the first $5,000 of the desired $15,000 the committee would like to raise. Four other prospects in the community are selected for personal solicitations. A committee member makes the four calls with the artistic director, taking photographs of the building as it now looks, a pencil sketch of the improvements, and a copy of the estimate. They explain that $20,000 (including the cash reserve) is already in hand for the renovations and that two committee members have already agreed to contribute $2,500 each toward the project. Three of the prospects agree to give, providing $7,500. A fourth gives $1,000, bringing the total from the four prospects to $8,500. At the end of the mini-campaign, when the $8,500 is combined with the two $2,500 contributions from committee members, only $1,500 has to be taken out of the emergency fund.

Note that in the example cited above, two of the six donations came from members of the board of trustees. In general, board members must be regarded as primary contributors (as noted in chapter 1) and should be asked to make a long-term financial commitment to the organization when they are invited to serve. Note also that, in this example, funds were being solicited for what is generally called a "one-time gift." A renovation project is unlikely to be repeated for many years, and for certain individuals the one-time gift may be appealing.

For contributors who are able to make sizable contributions every year (and most of those who can give one large gift are financially able to repeat the donation on an annual basis), a different approach should be tried. One successful organization has resorted to the practice of asking ten donors annually for a $2,000 contribution. The $2,000 figure was chosen because this is the cost of bringing one guest artist to perform with the resident chamber group. Each contributor is given the option of choosing a guest artist from a predetermined list and is encouraged to meet and dine with the performer during the residency period.

Above all, it is essential to keep in mind the obvious fact that $1,000 contributions add up a good deal faster than $25 donations. The statistics for many successful, community-based presenting organizations show that more than 80 percent of the amount contributed by individuals comes from fewer than 20 percent of the donors.

The larger donors should not only should be thanked for their gift but also given continued attention throughout the year. An invitation to tea with a performer or to a rehearsal; an informal, chatty note from the artistic director during the year; or other less formal indications of attention and appreciation are essential. Individual contributors must be nurtured so that their donations to your organization become a matter of habit.

RULE *31*

Remember your local BUSINESSES.

Too often arts organizations come to believe that attracting funds from businesses entails a major fund-raising effort aimed at one or two large firms. This technique is, more often than not, too costly for the long-term benefits gained. Occasionally a small organization will receive a substantial donation of several thousand dollars from a large, local business concern. All too often, however, the donation is made with the stipulation that it is a one-time gift. Remember that in fund raising, it is the ongoing donors who are the bread-and-butter support of the organization.

A sound approach to developing support is to seek small donations from many businesses in your community. The following is an example of this strategy:

> Year #1: The board of trustees drew up a list of all local business concerns, and individual board members indicated those with whom they did business or with whom they might have some influence or contact. A donation range was set up; businesses were told they could contribute from $75 to $250 (in three categories). In exchange they received a special listing in the program, with the larger contributors being listed at the top of the page in larger type. During the first round of soliciting (by personal appointments), thirty businesses agreed to participate for a total of $3,500 in contributions. Just before programs went to press, a letter went out to the businesses that had refused to donate the first time they were approached, giving them one more chance to do so. The letter listed those businesses which had given and would be listed in the program and encouraged the others to participate. After follow-up phone calls, fifteen more checks came in, increasing the total contributions to nearly $5,000. At the end of the season, all participating businesses received thank-you notes with a copy of the program enclosed.

Remember your local BUSINESSES.

> Year #2: All donating businesses from Year #1 received a reminder letter six months before the season started. They were reminded of their contribution from the previous year, given an opportunity to increase it, and told that they could either send their checks immediately or wait until the beginning of the season. The letter ended as follows: "Unless we hear from you, we will assume you will want to be listed again and the printer will be so instructed in preparing his copy." Meanwhile a list was made of other businesses that had not joined up. Specific members of the board were selected to encourage reluctant business executives. At the end of Year #2, sixty-seven businesses had contributed a total of $8,700.

This case history is instructive in several ways. First, although the initial work was considerable, the ultimate goal was an ongoing system to produce unrestricted funds—a system that required a mailing, a follow-up, and a minimal amount of new solicitation. Once such a system is set up, the support can be counted on year after year. Since the contributor pool is large, some cash will always be coming in, although the amount will fluctuate with business conditions.

Second, there is psychological advantage in setting both a lower and an upper limit to the amount that a small business may contribute. By keeping the lower limit at $75, which most businesses can afford, the courtesy $5 or $10 check is eliminated. Yet, by setting the upper limit at $250, business concerns need not feel that the organization is expecting too large a gift. Often executives refuse the organization's request, claiming that other community organizations, such as hospitals, the YMCA, and the Boy Scouts, make substantial demands and receive generous checks from them. If the arts organization stakes a very modest claim, there is usually an increased willingness to participate. After all, by being listed in the program, the business gets credit, at modest cost, for supporting the cultural life of the community.

Third, the arts organization is in a favorable position when competing businesses are located in the same town. Once one firm elects to make a contribution, the effective fund raiser must not be timid in pointing out to competitors what they are missing by not contributing. The business that has contributed is listed in the program. This tells potential customers in the audience that this public-spirited business supports the community and the presenting organization.

Finally, many local businesses often find themselves short of cash, but are willing to make contributions. In these cases, in-kind contributions may be accepted in lieu of cash. In the example just cited, contributions of flowers and gourmet foods were received. In the case of another organization that had to provide food and housing for musicians, several motels and restaurants donated food and lodging.

Other fund-raising techniques can be effective with local business concerns. Program sponsorship can bring in a large contribution and offer a business good exposure in exchange for a financial commitment. The business agrees to cover a predetermined amount of the cost of a performance in exchange for a specific type of crediting in the program and the publicity. In the case of underwriting, a business receives credit in exchange for a financial *guarantee against loss* on a particular event; if the event breaks even, the business pays nothing but still gets the credit. In many cases, businesses are willing to serve as sponsors or underwriters. It gives them unique exposure often with minimal risk and effort. For the presenting organization, either sponsorship or underwriting provides a kind of financial protection and, sometimes, a sizable contribution.

Many small presenting organizations believe that the best way to go after business support is to sell advertising in the printed program. But this technique needs to be examined carefully. Because they reach relatively small numbers of people, presenters cannot charge a great deal for advertising, and the extra printing costs eat up a lot of the money they do receive. The hours involved in selling the advertising should also be taken into account. Moreover, businesses that have agreed to take out an ad may be reluctant to give a contribution. Unless program ads are a proven lucrative source of support, it is probably best not to solicit them.

On the other hand, businesses can help the presenting organization in the area of advertising. They can offer the presenter exposure in their own regular ads. Because businesses buy so much advertising space in the local newspaper as well as advertising time on radio and television, they are occasionally willing to promote a presenter in one of their own ads. In one community, for example, the local bank announces the presenter organization's upcoming season in one of its weekly ads in the newspaper each year. The advertisement projects an image of a business enterprise concerned with the cultural affairs of the community—and this is done within the limits of the normal advertising budget. Many businesses like this kind of contribution because it costs them so little. Presenting organizations, in turn, are grateful for the free advertising that often gets premium placement.

RULE 32

If you must chase a rainbow, READ THIS SECTION.

Undoubtedly the most competitive fund raising in the United States of America is for the dollars of corporations and foundations. Although there are thousand of foundations, most are small and without professional staff, and the vast majority of their funds are not directed to the arts. Money from large corporations with professionally staffed giving programs has increased substantially over the last two decades, yet it too represents only a small portion of total giving to the arts, and most of that money goes to the most established organizations. Competition for dollars is intense; there is no question that of all the fund-raising marketplaces, corporations and private foundations are the most competitive.

Competition for dollars is only one issue that must be kept in mind in dealing with these sources. Another is the issue of program integrity. Occasionally compromises must be considered in order to attract funds from any major backer, but this is especially true when dealing with corporations, which generally want a lot of exposure, and private foundations, which generally have a specific giving agenda. Consider the following example:

> A presenter's chief fund raiser had finally succeeded in getting a luncheon date with a foundation president. During the course of the lunch, the fund raiser described the organization's activities and financial need. The foundation person listened politely, but with obvious lack of interest. After dessert he said, "Have you ever thought about including music students with the professionals in your programs? Our foundation is very interested in education. You know, if you were to come in with an application for a performance which included students and professionals together, I think we might be interested in helping you."

The above conversation poses a dilemma. Clearly, money is being offered, but there are strings attached. The conditions laid down could have an impact on the artistic integrity of the organization. The foundation representative is not to blame for specifying certain conditions—he has, in fact, been generous in giving an honest statement about what he can and cannot fund. If the sacrifices and compromises necessary are unacceptable, it is best to seek money elsewhere.

If you must chase a rainbow,
READ THIS SECTION.

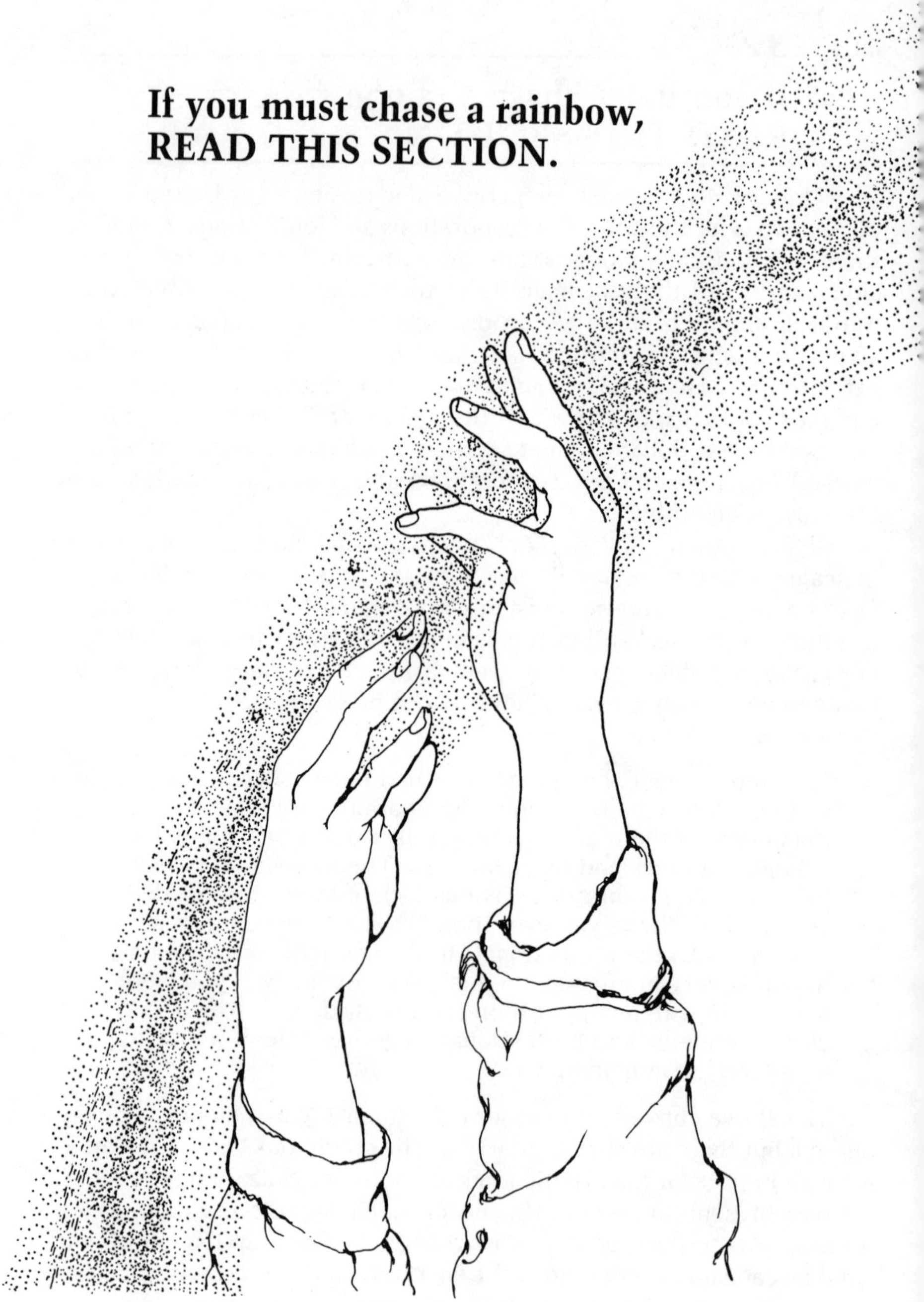

In soliciting from private institutional donors such as corporations and foundations, you need to follow certain rules. Seek money only for a specific project; do not ask for funds to support the ongoing work of the organization. Do not send in a formal application until someone from your organization has personally spoken to a representative. Corporations and foundations are flooded with appeals, and they generally send polite refusals to all those who request through the mail with no advance notice. Before talking with a representative of the funding source, try to find out about funding guidelines (larger foundations often have printed guidelines; corporations generally do not, but they do develop giving patterns). Once you know what a corporation or foundation might fund, look at your own operation to see whether there might be a fit with your activities. If you end up preparing a formal proposal, try to get a representative of the corporation or foundation to review a draft before it is formally submitted. In this way, you can troubleshoot problems and increase your chances of success by making changes in the final draft. The request itself should consist of the following:

1. a short cover letter on the organization's stationery stating that the enclosed material represents a formal request for funds (the letter should be signed by the board president or director);
2. a one- to three-page narrative description of the specific project which also gives basic information about the organization and its capability and track record;
3. a proposed budget; and
4. supporting documents, including the organization's brochure, resumes, programs, press material (a modest sampling is preferable to a huge amount).

These are a number of common mistakes made by organizations in applying to corporations and foundations. One is making numerous copies of a project proposal and sending these to many foundations or corporations, the names of which have been found in a reference book. This method is guaranteed to fail; instead, pick one or two potential sources on which to concentrate and try to arrange a meeting between a board member of your organization and an appropriate representative. A second common mistake is that of writing overly detailed, confused, or lengthy proposals. The clarity of a short narrative description and the credibility of the budget are of utmost importance. If detail is needed, you will be asked to supply it later.

If you are successful in receiving funds from a private foundation, be sure to mention this fact in your publicity and your programs. In addition, make an effort to keep the foundation people informed of

When dealing with public funding agencies, PERSEVERE.

your activities. Do not assume that foundation executives do not wish to be thanked personally. The organization should show its gratitude publicly (in publicity) and privately (by letter), regardless of whether it intends to seek funds from this source again.

RULE 33

When dealing with public funding agencies, PERSEVERE.

Be persistent in asserting your rights as a citizen when you approach public funding agencies. But remember, there are many other citizens!

There are several sources of public (governmental) funds. The National Endowment for the Arts (NEA) is the federal agency that supports organizations of regional and national significance and state arts agencies, often called "arts commissions" or "arts councils," which provide grants to a variety of constituents within their state borders. Besides the NEA, three other types of organizations also administer public funds and often work with presenters: regional (multistate) arts associations recognized and supported by the NEA (see appendix G); state arts agencies; and local—that is, city- or county-based—agencies and organizations.

The best place for a presenting organization to start in establishing a relationship with these various agencies is to contact the state arts agency. For the name, address, and telephone number of your state arts agency, contact the NEA or the National Assembly of State Arts Agencies in Washington, DC. A program officer at the state arts agency will explain the available options and may often direct the presenter to other organizations that might be able to provide advice, such as a presenter consortium in the area.

To apply for funds from a state arts agency, one must be familiar with the various programs through which grants can be awarded. Most agencies have a document, with a title such as "Guide to Programs," which gives the necessary program information together with application deadline dates and other pertinent facts. Read this material carefully before drafting a preliminary application. Also try to get an appointment with someone at the agency to discuss your situation. Often staff members hold meetings around the state, and you may be able to meet an agency representative at a location other than the state office. Invite agency staff people to your events. If no one from the agency can come to your area, go to the agency and ask for advice. It is important that the staff get to know you, your organization, and its work. Be persistent. It is your right as a citizen and taxpayer. Remember that you have a greater claim on employees of a public agency than you do on officers of private foundations. Be courteous but firm. Ask for advice and follow it to the extent possible. If your application is turned down the first time, call the agency and try to find out why. Ask for help in preparing another application. Do not become discouraged. Many organizations that are turned down initially have more success with their state arts agency the next time they apply.

There are several things to keep in mind in applying to a state arts agency. First, it is a government agency funded by federal and state tax revenues. As such, it is subject to the concerns of legislators and taxpayers and must be careful to show that it is not an elitist organization. It is therefore incumbent upon you to show in your application that your organization attempts to serve your entire community. If part of your program is directed toward schoolchildren, senior citizens, people of color, or the disabled, be sure to emphasize this in your application. If you have a specific project directed toward inner-city neighborhoods or rural settlements, perhaps this is the one for which you should be seeking funds. By doing so, you help the agency justify to state legislators and, ultimately, to the taxpayer, that the funds appropriated for the arts are being spent fairly.

Second, because the name with which you are probably most familiar at the state arts agency is the executive director's, it might seem logical to attempt to get an appointment with him or her. However, the executive director generally has a full schedule and is rarely the person administering the specific program under which you are applying. You are frequently better off getting an appointment with the appropriate program administrator, who can give you more time and can provide you with detailed information about your application.

Third, in filling out the application, be clear, concise, accurate, and brief. It should be typewritten, clearly legible, and without mistakes. Remember that, as a public agency, a state council is required to review every application it receives, and the volume of requests is tremendous. Applications that are bogged down with detail or are confusing stand a good chance of being set aside. Applications in which the numbers do not add up correctly will not receive a favorable reading. If you must include detail or supporting documents, do not attach them to the application itself, but label and refer to them as "Attachment A," "Attachment B," and so forth. If you are given the option of using extra sheets of paper to continue a narrative description of your project, try to avoid doing so. The sheer bulk and length of your application is not an index of its credibility. To those reviewing the application, it is much more impressive when a major program is cogently summarized, and more than a little frustrating to receive a fistful of programs, clippings, and descriptive prose.

Fourth, do not ignore the fact that many state arts agencies can provide your organization with various kinds of technical assistance, particularly in organizational development. Though the assistance generally involves a contribution of consultant time and services rather than a cash grant, good technical assistance can be extremely valuable. It is not uncommon to receive help in the areas of administration, promotion, and fund raising, for example. Some state arts councils regard this as a primary responsibility to their constituents.

Finally, remember your obligation to advocate for your state arts council and for its federal partner, the NEA. Just as you may be dependent on these organizations for support, so they are dependent on the actions of legislators at the state and national level. Consider it your responsibility to write regularly to your state and national representatives. When government funding has been used in a project, mention how important the event was in the cultural life of your community. Invite legislators to your own events. Act as an advocate to strengthen the concept of government support for the arts. Unless you as a citizen show strong support, you as a presenter will not get the money you want from the state arts agency because it will simply not be available.

As almost all readers of this book probably know, the National Endowment for the Arts is charged with the responsibility for making grants to individuals and organizations involved with the arts throughout the United States. Established by the U.S. Congress in the mid-1960s, the NEA has grown rapidly, though in recent years the pace of that growth has slowed considerably. As government agencies go, it is small; yet its impact on the arts has been immense. Many small arts organizations probably receive cash or services indirectly from the NEA without even being aware of it. Program funds for state arts councils come partially from the NEA; so do funds for numerous arts service organizations. (The publication of this book was made possible in part by a grant from the NEA.)

To many arts organizations, the NEA often seems like a giant monolith, a sprawling bureaucracy. Whether this perception is correct, it certainly is true that much frustration is often associated with direct appeals to the NEA for funds, particularly those made by organizations with modest budgets. The NEA is flooded with such applications and turns many down. Those that are successful often represent months or years of hard work, planning, and several previous rejections. A small organization should plan carefully before applying to the NEA. If an approach to this funding source is to be made, persistence bordering on doggedness is recommended. (A recommended procedure is described in appendix E.)

Presenting organizations are eligible to apply to many programs at the NEA so it is desirable to write to the agency (Washington, D.C., 20506) and request both its *Guide to Programs* as well as the booklet entitled *Program Information for Arts Presenters,* available from the Inter-Arts Office. Read these booklets carefully, pencil in hand, marking those programs to which you might apply. Then write again to the NEA requesting the guidelines for each of the programs you are interested in. These guidelines are more detailed and hence more useful than the composite guide.

Before you submit your official application, you should be in touch with your area's regional representative. This individual lives in your region and is responsible for making site visits to potential applicants, assisting them in applying, and giving them basic information on how the NEA works. (You can get the name and address of this person from your state arts agency.)

As with applications to state arts agencies, the application to the NEA should be clear and concise. Do not count on getting a grant. Do not make any commitments based on the expectation that funds will be forthcoming. Expect to be turned down the first time you apply. Remember that the NEA was not set up primarily to help every organization. It will take an interest in your organization only if you have an extremely compelling project.

Local arts agencies, connected with cities or counties, are also prospects for funding in many cases. In addition, your area may have a Department of Education, Community Action Program, Office of the Mayor, Human Relations Commission, Departments of Parks and Recreation, or some other entity that works with presenters. In smaller towns, public libraries, schools, and the town office itself should be solicited. (Civic clubs, though not municipal entities, are occasionally a source of funds.) All of these potential funding sources should be explored and you should make direct, personal solicitations and attempt to get a commitment of continuing support from year to year.

Conclusion

This chapter began with a description of the fantasy that lurks in the back of every fund raiser's mind: Somewhere, somehow, I will find someone who is very, very wealthy to support our organization. Somewhere, somehow, I will find a foundation or a government agency that has just been waiting to bestow money on us.

In the course of this chapter, I have tried to show how important it is to keep some perspective on that dream. Fund raising, like anything else, does not happen by itself. It is the result of careful planning, formulating convincing arguments for support, and putting in countless hours of hard work. Successful fund raisers know that their organizations are kept afloat by a large number of loyal contributors, most of whom are individuals who donate money year after year. If your organization has not yet gotten itself organized for effective fund raising, get busy: there is much work to be done. There is a large potential constituency in your local community. Work on individuals, small businesses, and your state arts agency; seek ongoing, dependable relationships with them. If you develop this kind of support, you will weather the economic storms that imperil other arts organizations, and you can look forward to many successful seasons.

Don't buy a RUBE GOLDBERG!

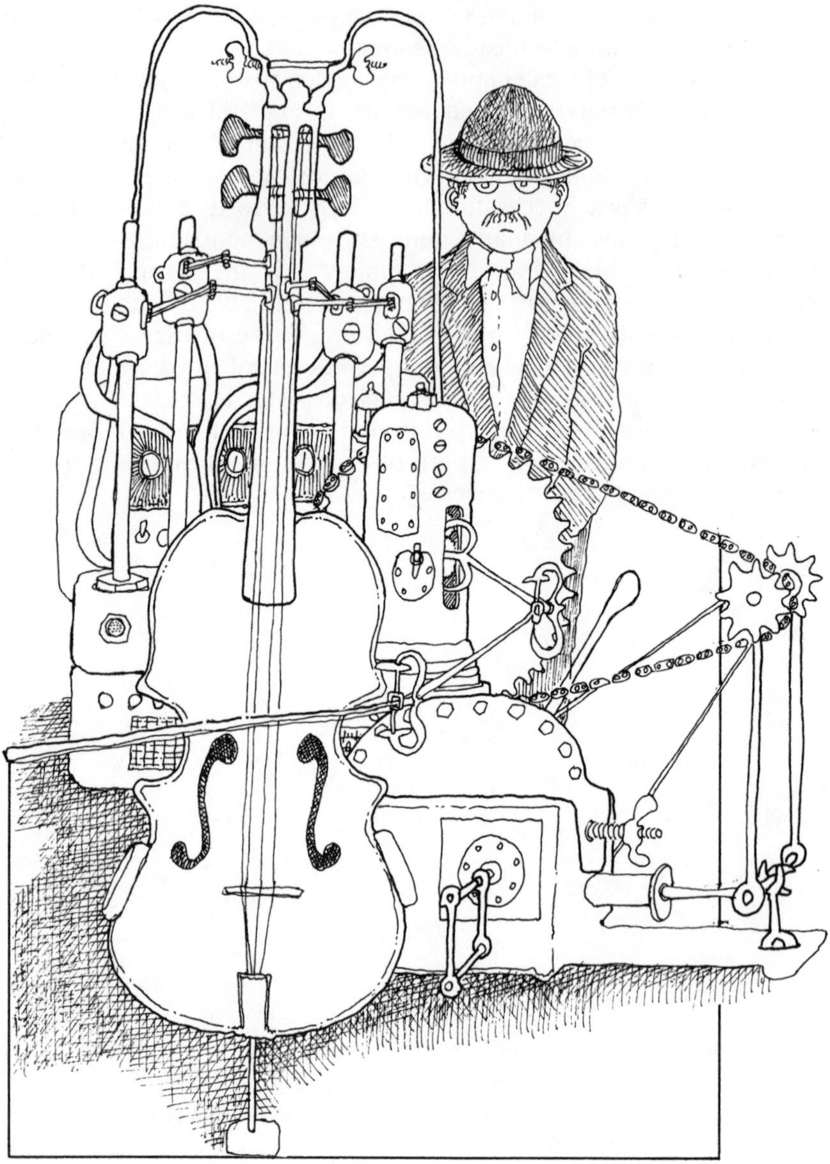

5

Behind the Curtain

"Let's have a dance, theater, or opera company next season. We have always talked about doing something big."

or

"How about an outdoor festival next summer? We could have a 'street theater' all over town and a special event in the park."

These are familiar words to anyone who has spent much time with a presenting organization. Almost always someone wants to bring in more ambitious productions or put on performances in outdoor locations. Chamber music or a solo concert is fine, they argue, but it appeals to a narrow group of music lovers. What is really needed is either something grand and elaborate or something outdoors which is fun. For the winter series, these people may suggest a performing group that can attract a large audience—a Balinese dance group, a Gilbert and Sullivan operetta, a Shakespearean theater troupe, or maybe Verdi's

Aida. For the summer series, they may urge the selection of a bluegrass band, a children's theater ensemble, or even a small-scale circus that can perform on the Town Green. The basic argument is simple: such events appeal to a broader audience, which makes it easier to raise money and sell tickets.

The argument is not unreasonable, but the presenting organization must think carefully about two issues: the cost of such events and their technical requirements. Most presenters are wise enough to ask how much such events will cost, but many do not realize that this question cannot be answered without knowing how much time, effort, and money will have to be expended for equipment and technical staff. They also overlook the immense drain on time and energy that large productions can represent for presenting organizations. A large touring company may have many logistical and technical problems which require more expertise, organization, time, and patience than the staff and the board can spare. Outdoor productions offer many problems, not the least of which is the unpredictability of weather and the additional worries of postponement or relocation or both.

This chapter concerns some of the important technical considerations that help to determine how much time, effort, and money specific kinds of performances require. It includes advice on how to avoid technical disasters, how to plan for indoor or outdoor extravaganzas, and how to remain calm and confident in the most trying of preperformance situations. As always, the key requirement is good planning and a realistic appraisal of what you and your organization can manage to accomplish.

RULE 34

Don't buy a RUBE GOLDBERG!

Let us start with the obvious. If you want to avoid a technical nightmare, you can help yourself immensely by not hiring a performing group that will, by its very nature and complexity, offer a host of insurmountable technical problems. Some large touring productions require little technical equipment or expertise from presenters. They are self-contained packages needing only a large performing space. Other touring shows, even some that are otherwise remarkably modest, seem like the classic "Rube Goldberg" as far as their technical requirements are concerned. Complex and intricate, they call for a great deal of expertise, labor, and equipment supplied by the presenting organization.

How does a presenting organization figure out whether it can manage and afford these demanding productions? Obviously, as a first step the organization must find out exactly what it is buying. Someone with technical and production knowledge must carefully evaluate the technical responsibilities of the presenter before a contract is signed. This information is essential regardless of the size of the company or the type of production. Indeed, almost any touring performer or group will require some technical help. Even a small chamber ensemble will probably require a clean, properly-heated stage area; chairs and music stands; a tuned piano; adequate toilet facilities; and a stage manager. When the technical requirements are modest, they may or may not be spelled out in the contract (if you do not find any there, ask the booking agent or a member of the group). With larger touring attractions, technical requirements are almost always spelled out on separate pages called technical "riders" or "spec sheets." Many presenters initial these riders without understanding what they mean. Don't do it. As always, read the fine print.

If you want to avoid buying a "Rube Goldberg," you should find out whether the large performing group you are considering has done a lot of touring. If it has, ask for a list of other presenters who have hired the group and find out from them what the costs were, how much equipment had to be supplied, how flexible the performing group's technical people were, how many work-hours the presenting organization had to contribute. If the performing group has not done a lot of touring, beware. Never consider performers simply because you have seen them do impressive productions in their own theater. Touring, particularly the touring of "one-nighters," is a special kind of operation. Setups must be done in a matter of hours, not days. A local, often inexperienced, crew must be trained without the luxury of many rehearsals. Local equipment may be less than ideal and will vary from night to night. Touring equipment breaks down and must be repaired or replaced. An excellent company without touring experience may be unrealistic about all these factors when it puts shows on the road for the first time. All too often, the technical staff expects excellent performance facilities and expert crews. The more experienced touring groups know that such expectations are unrealistic.

Finally, if you want to avoid the pitfalls of a technical disaster, keep your end of the bargain. If the stage crew is your responsibility, make sure that the proper number of stagehands is at the auditorium on time. If you have promised to hang some lights before the group arrives, be sure this gets done. The performing group is depending on you. If you meet your obligations, it is more likely that you can keep costs in line and enjoy a trouble-free performance.

The essence of a good relationship between presenter and performing group is effective communication. Obviously, this depends on

Know your SPACE.

a dialogue in which both sides ask questions and understand what the answers to their questions really mean. In the remaining sections, we review some of the questions you can expect from the performing group and other questions that you should be asking in return.

RULE 35

Know your SPACE.

The first questions you should be prepared to answer concern your performing space. If it is an indoor location, is it a high school auditorium, church, concert hall, theater, or gym? Does it have a stage? If so, what kind (for example, proscenium, thrust, or arena)? What are the stage dimensions? What type of floor does it have? Is there an orchestra pit? What kind of lighting exists? What are the backstage facilities like? Is yours a union house? These are all basic questions that should determine to a large extent what kinds of performing groups you can consider.

It is probably a good idea to develop a technical specifications packet concerning your facility which answers these questions. This can save you a great deal of work. If you do not have such a document, you will end up having to fill out technical questionnaires each time a touring company plans to perform in your facility. Once you have prepared the answers to key questions, you will have fulfilled most of the informational requirements for any performing group that you hire. Where additional information is required, the performing group will ask. (To figure out what questions need to be answered, either get a technical information packet from an experienced presenter or request a technical information questionnaire from an experienced touring group.)

Knowing about the performing space is important, whether you are considering a solo performer or a large company. For example, a recorder soloist needs a relatively small auditorium with good acoustics: a gym would be totally inappropriate. If your facility does not have a stage, do not despair; rather, choose the performing group carefully. Some touring attractions require only a "four-wall rental" without a stage (that is, a large open space with adequate seating and electrical power). They are sufficiently versatile to put on a convincing performance in almost any location. But increasingly, larger companies are becoming more discriminating about where they perform, particularly as the number of adequate performing spaces is increasing.

There are several kinds of stages, and you should become knowledgeable about what you have. The three basic stage types are proscenium, thrust, and arena. The most familiar is the proscenium stage, in which the stage area is separated completely from the audience by the proscenium arch and, usually, a curtain. The audience looks at the stage from one direction, and the action on stage is directed through the proscenium opening. A thrust stage is generally surrounded by the audience on two or three sides, whereas an arena stage offers a theater-in-the-round, with the audience completely surrounding the stage area.

Most large touring attractions are intended for proscenium stages. Scenery is designed so that the action will play downstage (in front). (This same scenery will obscure the view of some members of the audience if it is placed on an arena stage.) Stage action is "blocked" so that performers face out and are downstage when important action or lines are required. Lighting is set up so that performers are adequately lit from one direction only—much simpler than having to light adequately for many different audience positions. If backstage activity is vital, if performer exits and entrances are numerous, a proscenium stage, with its backstage area well masked from the audience's view, may be the only kind that the performing group can use. Any presenting organization that does not have a proscenium theater must be sure that the performing group can put on a good show in the space available.

Stage dimensions vary and so do the requirements of touring productions. One touring opera group, for example, requests as a minimum a stage with 25 feet from the back wall to the curtain line, 36 feet in stage width, and no less than 14 feet in stage height. If the group carries an orchestra, it will need a pit area in front of the stage (dimensions vary with the number of players). Although dance troupes are also concerned with stage dimensions, they are equally interested in having an adequate floor. For a dancer, the floor is a part of the performing instrument. It allows the dancer to give the proper physical expression to the body by supplying the proper resilience and slickness. Nonresilient floors like concrete are actually dangerous for dancers, and you must be sure not only that the floor surface is wood but that it is not laid directly over concrete or supported by metal piers which allow no floor movement. If the dance troupe seems worried about your floor surface, get in touch with a local dancer and have this individual check out the floor carefully.

In addition to the stage area, the performing group will require adequate backstage facilities. Again, this applies as much to a solo performer as it does to a large group, although the exact needs of each may differ. A backstage area without a toilet is a hardship, and many contracts require both a toilet and a sink with hot and cold running water. A large troupe will also require dressing rooms. In gymnasiums, locker rooms are often adequate if they are near the stage area and have no public access during the performance. Some groups are flexible and will work with what you have. But be sure to tell them what to expect before they arrive and, preferably, before you sign the contract.

A large company will have numerous other items to check out before it arrives. Often, these items are covered in your technical information packet or in a questionnaire that the more experienced groups send out as a matter of course. If you don't have a technical information packet, you must take the performers' questionnaires very seriously. If they are filled out accurately and completely, the technical staff of the company can evaluate your particular setup in great detail before the group arrives. A performing group is almost always under severe time pressure when a setup is involved, and the company's technical people should not have to discover the idiosyncracies of your space after they arrive. If your facility has a "technical director," let this person handle the technical liaison with the performing group.

In this connection, it is essential that you be completely frank, honest, and precise about all details of your facility. Glossing over inadequacies or "estimating" the technical specifications will almost always lead to trouble. Technical deficiencies can often be dealt with if a performing group knows about them well in advance. If they have adequate lead time, many companies have a good track record in meeting the challenges of facilities that are under par. Similarly, performers can be warned by the company's staff if they will encounter less than ideal backstage or on-stage conditions. But if the performers or company technical staff discover problems at the last minute, the performance quality will often suffer, there will be hard feelings, and, on occasion, you will end up having to pay more money.

RULE 36

Hire RELIABLE technical help.

Many presenters expend a lot of energy selecting excellent performing groups but are fairly casual about hiring technical help. Their attitude seems to be, "anyone will do." Inadequate technical help can mar an otherwise excellent performance. Consider the following example:

> A touring opera company arrives in town with its own staff of four well-trained technicians. A crew of fourteen local people, assembled somewhat haphazardly by the presenter, is waiting to help them set up and run the show. Among the local crew members are five students. At 1 p.m. they help unload the company truck but at 2:30 they go off to an afternoon class.

Hire RELIABLE technical help.

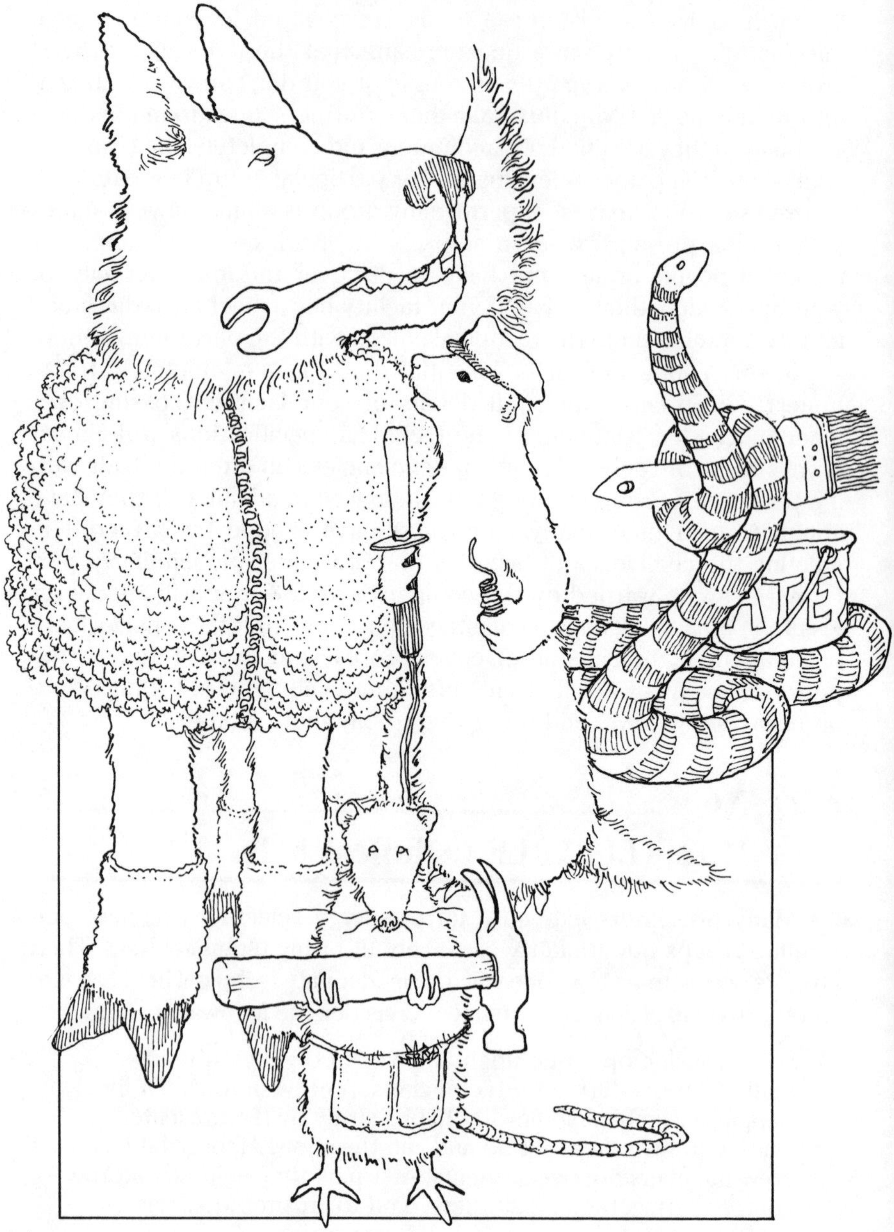

They return at 5. Because they have not been a part of the setup, they do not really understand how the scene changes will work during the show, and the company's chief technician decides to give them simple jobs that do not require a great deal of explanation. One student is assigned to curtain pulling. However, at 7 p.m. he decides to go out with friends and gets another student to fill in for him. In explaining the curtain cue (a warning light turned on, followed by a curtain-pull light turned off), he gets the instructions reversed. During the performance, 45 seconds before the end of the first act, the warning cue is given but is mistaken for the curtain-pull cue. The curtain closes just before the tenor and soprano sing their final high C's—the most important vocal moment of the entire first act.

Although not all examples are so dramatic, others show how important it is to hire responsible and reliable people who will care about the quality of their work. Any experienced touring group can tell you stories about local crews who damaged valuable equipment, talked loudly backstage during the performance, arrived two hours late for setup, or "forgot" that they were responsible for a load-out after the show and walked away with some of the company's equipment instead.

Clearly it is in your interest to hire reliable help. If the local crew is union, you have no control over who will work. The business agent of the local office will supply the workers. In other cases, however, if hiring the crew is your responsibility, take it seriously. Here are some rules you should follow:

1. If your facility has a technical director or building manager, this person should be consulted when a crew is hired and should be paid to be on site during the entire time the company is in residence. If such a person is not available, another individual must be selected who knows where all equipment is stored, has the authority to make decisions, and has keys to every room.
2. If you hire a student crew, be sure that the same students will be available for the entire load-in, setup, and working of the show.
3. Try not to hire temperamental people for your stage crew (prima donnas belong on the stage, not behind it). The technical staff of the touring group will be under great pressure and should be given willing, cooperative people with whom to work.
4. Make certain that your crew members arrive ON TIME for the crew "call" (the time set for unloading the truck). Nothing is more frustrating than a short crew (fewer people than requested) at precisely the time when many helpers are needed.
5. Find out from the touring group how much technical expertise is needed among your crew members. In many cases, you will find

Know the UNION rules.

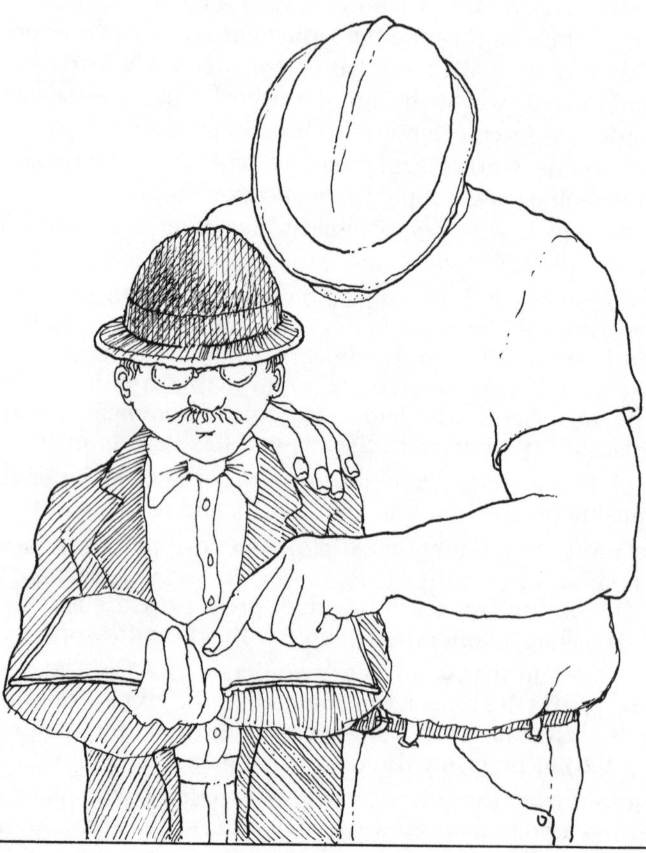

that willing and able-bodied novices are suitable. If not, be sure you provide people with the proper technical know-how.

6. If your facility presents special load-in or setup problems, ask the technical representative of the performing group whether the company will require additional local crew members. The performing group is making an assumption that your facility is not out of the ordinary and that load-in and setup will be normal. Some load-ins are not straightforward, however. Some facilities require forklifting equipment or the carrying of scenery up a flight of stairs, for example, and these special situations require either additional helpers or an earlier crew call so that the company's tight setup schedule can be met.

RULE 37

Know the UNION rules.

Sometimes presenting organizations decide to put on their gala event in a large, downtown auditorium with plenty of seats; only after the decision is made do they discover that the auditorium is a union house. Often this means unexpected stagehand and musician expenses. Even if the presenting group is careful to choose a house over which the various unions do not have direct jurisdiction, the touring group itself may have a unionized technical staff. If this is the case, the performing company generally has an agreement with the technical staff's unions requiring that local workers from the same unions be hired. In some cases, the company may be required to work with "loaders" from the local Teamsters' Union to unload and reload the company's truck.

The best way to avoid union problems is to understand why they occur. Several unions are connected with the performance business, and each has its own rules. The presenter should be familiar with three categories of unions: musicians, stagehands, and loaders. Here is what you should know about each.

UNIONS

MUSICIANS, SINGERS, DANCERS. Most touring instrumentalists belong to the American Federation of Musicians (AFofM), whereas singers and dancers often belong to the American Guild of Musical Artists (AGMA). In general, neither union will deal directly with the presenter. However, in certain large, downtown performing spaces, the local office of the AFofM may have "jurisdiction." This means that a certain specified number of local union members must be hired for every performance. If no musicians are needed (as in the case of theatrical productions), or if the performing group brings in its own musicians from outside the union local, the presenting organization may find that it has to pay "house" musicians from the union local. In certain cases, the presenting organization may be able to work out a compromise with the business office of the union but only if negotiations begin before the performing space has been definitely confirmed.

You should also be aware that it is a common procedure for the local office of the AFofM to demand "work dues" from any players from outside the union local who come in to perform and are playing within its jurisdiction. Thus, if you hire a group from out of town, even in an auditorium without "house" musician arrangements, you may see a representative from the local union at performance time. In this case, remember that he or she is there to speak with the musicians, not with you. Work dues are a local union's tax on players, and in no case should you expect to pay them.

STAGEHANDS AND WARDROBE PERSONNEL. There are two situations in which presenters are likely to work with union stagehands and wardrobe personnel: when their performances take place in a union "house" (facility) and when the touring company travels with its own union stagehands. The arrangement with a union house is generally straightforward, and your dealings will be with the technical director of that facility. However, in nonunion houses, the issues are less clear when the incoming group uses union personnel. Because most touring companies will not carry all of their own technical help and will specify how many local helpers are needed, the presenter will have to bring in local stagehands to help. If the company is unionized, all or some of the people who are hired locally will probably have to be members of the union as well.

Obviously, this has practical ramifications for presenters because in almost every case, it is the local presenting organization that has to pay the local crew. If there is a requirement that these people be union members, the costs can rise substantially. In some presenting organizations, in which regular nonunion stage crew, maintenance staff, or students may be available, the cost for a union crew can be as much as triple that of a nonunion crew. The goal for the presenter should be to get the best job done for the least amount of money. Often, however, the presenter has no choice about whether to use union or nonunion personnel. That determination depends upon the incoming performing group's contractual relationship with the unions.

Though union crews are almost always more expensive than nonunion crews, figuring out the difference in cost may not be a simple matter. The performing group generally specifies what kind of technical help it needs and how many people it will take to get the job done, but it cannot guarantee the exact number of hours it will take to complete the work. In some cases, a local presenter who has access only to individuals with little experience will end up paying for many more work-hours than would be the case with an experienced crew—union or nonunion.

The principal stagehands' union is the International Alliance of Theatrical Stage Employees (IATSE). If the events in a series use unionized performing groups, the presenter will generally end up dealing with union stagehands provided by the local IATSE office. The local is contacted by a performing group, which sends out a so-called "yellow card" to the business agent of each local union in whose jurisdiction it will be performing. The yellow card announces the show; gives the date, time, and location of the setup and performances; and requests a certain number of stage carpenters, electricians, people to handle props, and others. If the yellow card is sent—and touring union crews must send it or face stiff fines—most presenters can usually expect a full union crew.

Clearly, then, one of the most important questions to ask potential touring companies is: are you a "yellow-card company"? If the answer is yes, be sure to estimate the cost of your union stagehands carefully before signing the contract. Remember, too, that many fine groups are available that travel with nonunion stage help. If you engage one of these, be sure to attach to the contract a rider stipulating that the performing group is not a yellow-card company and that, should it become one between the time the contract is signed and the performance date, the company will be responsible for paying the difference between union scale and local nonunion wages.

Does a yellow-card company always work with a local union crew? The preceding discussion suggests that it does; so do the rules of the stagehands' unions. In reality, however, a number of compromises have been worked out between local presenting organizations and the business agents of union locals. If you live outside an urban area, for example, it is likely that the local is small and that many of the members are film projectionists with steady jobs who do not wish to take a night off to work with the incoming group. On a busy night in any area of the country, there may not be enough union stagehands to cover all the work. The business agent may be willing to allow you to hire your own nonunion crew; or the agent may suggest that you hire one or two union workers and fill out the crew with your own nonunion people (students, friends, janitorial staff); or the local may be willing to issue temporary permits to allow your own workers to work at a lower rate, though you will still have to pay into the union's health and welfare fund. Do not assume that the union will be unreasonable. In many cases, workable compromises have been arranged which guarantee the presenting organization some good union help assisted by an inexperienced student crew. But remember that these arrangements must be worked out well ahead of performance day, preferably before a contract is signed with the performing group.

LOADERS. According to strict union definitions, stagehands are not supposed to load or unload a truck, although in most cases they do. This work is supposed to be done by loaders who are members of the Teamsters' Union. In many auditoriums around the country, Teamster loaders never appear. But in larger cities and even in some smaller communities, union loaders may be required.

The situations that determine whether loaders will appear are similar to those of union stagehands. They can appear when the auditorium is union-controlled; or they may sometimes appear if the touring company's union truck driver sends out a notification to the local Teamsters' office about the company's performance. However, even if the driver does that, it is not certain that any loaders will appear. If loaders do arrive on the scene, your contract with the performing group will probably specify that your organization must pay them.

The unexpected appearance of loaders can be financially devastating to a presenting organization. Not only are their work rates high, but they must often be paid for a certain minimum number of hours regardless of how long they actually work. For example, it is not unheard-of to pay a couple of loaders for a four-hour "in" (unload) and a four-hour "out" (reload) when the work itself only takes 45 minutes each way. Because loader bills can mount up quickly, it is essential to know whether loaders will appear before you make any firm plans to book a particular performing group in a specific theater.

The easiest way to make sure that you will not have loaders is to hire a nonunion company for a nonunion house, though there is always a chance that the company will have a union truck driver who will call for union loaders. If you do bring in a yellow-card company, check the contract carefully to see whether there is a provision for loaders. If there is, ask the booking agent whether the company's truck driver is a Teamster. If he is not, and if you are careful to avoid a union-controlled hall in your area, you will probably not experience any difficulties.

RULE 38

Supply proper equipment that WORKS.

The only way to know what equipment you must supply is to ask the company before you sign the contract. Find out what the power requirements are, how many lighting instruments (lamps, gels, and dimmers) will be needed, how much cable and masking is required, and what type of sound system the company is requesting. Once you have made a commitment to supply equipment, you are obligated to provide, in good working order, items that correspond closely to the exact specifications given by the company.

In outdoor performance spaces, the power requirements are especially important. In estimating power needs, remember that outdoor lighting requires a great deal of current. You should evaluate a performing group's technical specifications with this in mind. If sufficient standing power is unavailable, you will have to resort to generators. These can sometimes be obtained free or for a nominal charge from highway, public works, or fire departments. Generators tend to be noisy and give off unpleasant odors, so a downwind location is a must (the power capability of the generator plus the gauge of the electrical cable will determine just how far from the performing space the machine can be stationed). Generators seem to be temperamental at times and require constant care and fueling. It may be a good idea to station someone near your generator for security and fueling purposes.

Other kinds of equipment, particularly lighting and sound equipment not carried by the performing group, must be borrowed, rented, or purchased. Many presenting organizations gradually build up the technical equipment in their auditoriums by purchasing items that can be amortized over several years and many productions. If, for example, several shows a month require lighting, it may be wise to look into the possibility of purchasing lighting equipment, especially if the cost of rental is high and equipment is sometimes difficult to find. Sound equipment is generally easier to rent and, because presenters may need to hire a sound technician anyway, it is often sensible to secure the person and equipment as a package.

In larger cities and towns, theatrical rental houses can meet the needs of local presenters needing additional equipment. However, rental equipment is often delivered late, delivery can be expensive, and, most important, rental equipment is seldom kept in good repair. It is common, for example, to find essential parts missing from complicated machinery. For all these reasons, the presenting organization must

Supply proper equipment that WORKS.

check carefully into the reputations of the rental firms it deals with. If a local auditorium has the equipment you need, try borrowing or renting from this source first (you can at least test the equipment and transport it yourself). If, instead, you do end up dealing with a rental firm, have someone with technical expertise check the equipment, and call several times in advance to verify the delivery date and time.

Although performing groups will probably specify the equipment they would like to use, most will be flexible if you are unable to supply all of it. Occasionally one piece of equipment can be substituted for another, or the technical requirements can be simplified or changed. But in fairness to the technical staff, give plenty of advance warning if you are running into difficulties. Do not wait until the company's arrival to inform them that they will not be receiving what they asked you to supply.

RULE 39

For open space performances, consider DESERT ISLANDS and TIMES SQUARE.

Open space events—those that take place outdoors or in large areas like shopping malls or train stations—are the backbone of arts programming for presenters who wish to take the performers to the audience rather than wait for the audience to come to the performers. In many cases, they include some exciting and important presentations that reach a broad spectrum of people. But they also can offer a host of technical problems, and it is good to think carefully about these in the early planning stages.

The first issue in thinking about using an open space is making sure there is a good match between the space and the performers you are considering hiring. Some presenters choose the space first and then look for the performers. In other cases, it is done the other way around. Whichever technique is used, it is essential to ensure compatibility between performer and space. Many music groups cannot perform in an outdoor space that does not have special covering to protect instruments from sun and rain. In noisier spaces, dance performances may be more successful than theater presentations or intimate chamber music concerts.

With good planning, though, the imaginative use of space can itself be part of a good performance. Presenters have used outdoor steam pipes as backdrops for dance performances, and one presenter actually made space available in a pool for her audience for a hot summer performance. Malls have become popular spaces in recent years, though one generally has to arrange with the management beforehand

For open space performers, consider DESERT ISLANDS and TIMES SQUARE.

to shut off the electronic sound system which pipes background music throughout the space at most times.

In choosing a space, you must select a location that your potential audience can find easily. Try to avoid locations for which detailed directions or maps are necessary. In public spaces, you must be sure that your event will pose no potential conflicts with others who may have a prior claim upon the space. Generally, the city or town will have an agency that provides permits (for example, most municipal park departments issue "park-use" permits). Downtown spaces can be checked with city hall, the chamber of commerce, or, in smaller towns, with the town manager's office. Vacant lots must be cleared with their owners, private or public. In all cases you should get written permission guaranteeing you certain rights in the use of the space during performance time.

Before making a final decision on your space, estimate carefully the number of people you expect to attend the event. Determine whether there is adequate seating close enough to the performance area so that the audience will be able to see and hear comfortably. Sound diffuses quickly out-of-doors, especially when there is wind, so be conservative about how far performers' voices or instruments will carry without an electrical sound system. You must also determine whether your audience will be seated in chairs or on the grass, or be forced to stand during the performance. If the ground around the stage area is not grassy and clean, you should probably provide chairs. If the performance is long, seating is a virtual necessity. However, if your performance is within the context of a festival or bazaar and the audience feels free to come and go, seating need not be provided.

In choosing an open space, you must also consider crowd control. If admission is charged, entrance locations must be restricted. Many open spaces, such as fairgrounds and stadiums, that are commonly used for paying customers are designed carefully with containment in mind. Not only does this limit the number of "crashers"—people trying to get in free—but it allows the presenting group to control the number of people entering the space at any particular time. This may be especially important if the space has a legal restriction on capacity. If you are selecting a space that is not designed in this fashion, think carefully about how you can judiciously place barriers and people to control the flow of your audience. Regardless of the format, open-space performances require staff and volunteers to monitor crowd control and public safety.

Events presented in open spaces are almost always more unpredictable than performances in theaters. This is one reason why the most skillful open-event planners become fully familiar with every aspect of their space. They work with maps on which they have marked the flow of traffic and people. Outdoor-event planners may even indicate the sun's position and movement so that performance spaces can be set up without the sun blinding either audience or performers, a severe problem in the early morning or late afternoon. They know the location of emergency exits, fire hydrants, and other safety equipment. They have figured out the most judicious places to station security and volunteers. When the event actually takes place, they have an exact sense of how the space will be used throughout the performance period.

Outdoor stages present unique problems that must be worked out ahead of time. Aside from the usual considerations (dimensions, floor, and so forth), stages constructed for outdoor events must be tested to ensure that they are level, and their height must be carefully planned with the eye level of the audience in mind. Stage backing is usually provided both for visual and acoustical reasons. The best backing for concerts and other performances in which sound projection is critical is an acoustical shell. Should this not be available, you can use fabric to mask visual distractions behind the stage and to provide maximum sound projection. Be sure to test the background on a windy day to make certain that it is properly anchored. The stage should be placed in a location as sheltered from the wind as possible.

The general stage area must be accessible by car and truck if any equipment is to be brought in, and there must be secure areas behind the stage to store equipment. If no dressing rooms are close by, think about renting a trailer or enclosed truck, which can be parked behind the stage and used by the performers. Even if performers have no costume changes or can be convinced to change into costume at another location, it is desirable to have a portable rest room in back of the stage area for their exclusive use. Off-stage areas on either side of the performing space should be masked with canvas tarps and ropes so that performers' entrances and exits are hidden from the audience's view.

Experienced presenters who work outdoors a lot know that there are special techniques for dealing with the unpredictability of weather. They make sure they have plenty of sheets and tarpaulins to protect equipment from rain in case they have misjudged the sky. They use electrical equipment that is watertight. They make sure everything is properly anchored in case of high winds. If the day is clear but windy, they make sure that microphones are equipped with wind shields to prevent "whistling" and that clothespins or clamps are provided with the music stands so that sheet music does not blow away.

Presenters of outdoor events must decide early on whether postponement is possible or preferable to an indoor performance at an alternative location in case of inclement weather. If suitable alternative locations are unavailable and if the entire spirit of the event might be compromised if it is held indoors, it is a good idea to check to see whether the performing group would be prepared to accept postponement. Be prepared: a touring group on a tight itinerary will not accept the engagement under such chancy conditions. However, if the performing group is willing, make sure you have fully explained your procedure for postponement decisions. Include a rider in the contract such as the one below:

Sample Rider

> All performances will take place outdoors. In the case of inclement weather the presenter reserves the right to postpone performances. Postponement decisions will be made by the presenter at least 6 hours before the scheduled performance, and it will be the responsibility of the performer to make contact with the presenter before the performance (phone numbers below). A postponed performance will be rescheduled at the convenience of both parties.

RULE ***40***

Be PREPARED.

Be prepared! It's the Boy Scout's watchword. From all available evidence, however, many presenters were never Boy Scouts. Ask the technical staff of a touring company what is the most common problem on the road and you will probably be told: "We never seem to get a full crew at the time of the load-in. People do eventually dribble in, but we end up unloading the truck ourselves." If you press the point, you may be told that the second most common problem is having to work with a space that has not been adequately cleared of scenery and debris from an earlier production. Consider the following account:

> The crew call for a touring theater company setup had been set for 1:00 p.m. at a college in Pennsylvania. The company's truck driver and crew had driven through the night from Ohio, checked into a motel at 7:00 a.m., got a few hours of sleep, and arrived at the facility at 12:30 p.m. No one was around. The building was locked. Large cans, apparently filled with trash and debris, were sitting on the loading dock. The presenter, the head of the college's Humanities Department, was in a class and could not be reached until 2:00. After much searching, someone who had a key let the technical staff into the building. Walking into the facility, the four individuals gazed with horror at the remains of a circus

Be PREPARED.

that had been in the building the night before. There were no seats in the auditorium. Equipment was stacked on the stage and backstage. The room was full of paper trash and soft drink bottles. Worst of all, no one seemed to know anything about a local crew. In desperation, the technical staff attempted to clear the loading dock and unload the company truck. Much to their dismay, they found that the large cans on the dock were filled with animal defecation and that the trash department was not scheduled to clear the area until 4:00 p.m.

It is largely as a result of situations like this one that touring companies have put riders into their contracts like the one below:

Sample Rider

The company will carry its own technical staff. The company will request, in advance, additional workers (stagehands, loaders, and unloaders) in the numbers required for the setup, performance, and strike of the show. In the past this has usually amounted to an additional _____ persons. Local auspices are responsible for paying these workers.

If the number of additional stagehands as specified to the business agent of the local stagehands' union or directly to the auspices is not going to be present at the time of unloading, working the show and loading, the crew of the company will engage additional personnel; and the auspices will be responsible for paying these additional people at $100.00 per person, up to the number specified.

Exactly what does this rider mean? If the company has requested a local crew of fourteen at 1:00 p.m. and only twelve show up, then the technical staff can hire two additional people (members of the company's administrative staff, performers, or others), and the presenter will be responsible for paying each of these individuals $100 for their work. If the presenter has not bothered to hire any crew members—and, believe it or not, this sometimes occurs—the company can legally submit a stagehands' bill of $1,400. Obviously, it is better for both the presenter and the performing group if a full crew shows up on time and the stage area is cleared and ready for setup.

There are other ways for presenters to be prepared for the performing group's technical staff. Often presenters commit themselves to supplying various kinds of sound and lighting equipment. Once this commitment is made, it is necessary to verify that the equipment will be delivered or be available when needed. Do not assume, for example, that just because your auditorium is supplied with the necessary lighting instruments the performing group will be permitted to use them. Check with the building manager or technical director and get permission to use the equipment; make sure this person is available to answer questions when the technical staff of the company arrives. If equipment is to be delivered to the auditorium, call the supplier several times to verify that it is ordered or has been sent, and make sure that someone is at the auditorium to receive and sign for it.

Being prepared for the performing group also entails making certain that all prehanging has been carried out according to the company's instructions before the crew's arrival. It is common, for example, for a company to send a light plot ahead so that lights can be hung before the official crew call. If the presenter does not carry out this prehanging, the time pressure on the technical staff becomes severe and, in some cases, unpleasant compromises must be made. If a light plot that is totally unworkable in your auditorium is sent to you, call the technical representative of the company immediately. Reasonable changes can be made in plenty of time to get the hanging carried out on schedule. Do not, however, make any changes in the lighting plan or in any other prehanging instructions without discussing them with the company representative so that the technical staff knows what to expect upon arrival.

Finally, being prepared for the performing group means being ready to handle any unforeseen complications during the day of the performance. Give the company several telephone numbers to call so that some member of your organization will be available to give immediate answers to specific questions. Even if a company member does not call, go to the auditorium during the morning of the group's arrival to make sure everything is ready. Once the technical staff has arrived and has started to work, return to the auditorium and make sure things are going smoothly. Your interest and help will be appreciated and ultimately may contribute to a trouble-free performance.

Conclusion

Part of the magic of attending a performance as a member of the audience is that one does not know what goes on behind the curtain. In large productions, scenery and lighting changes seem to occur automatically at the proper moments. We can be shifted from a bedroom to a country scene in a matter of minutes. In less lavish productions, even those involving only one or two musicians, we do not see the instrument cases, the street clothes, or the water glasses stored backstage; we are treated to a performance. In a way, this is one of the things that makes a performing arts event so special. Behind the curtain, performers are not out of the ordinary (they are tired or thirsty or worried about the rent check); in front, they become important participants in an event that stretches our imaginations, makes us enlightened, happy, or sad.

This chapter has been called "Behind the Curtain" because the curtain is a somewhat arbitrary barrier between two worlds—the world of lighting equipment, dressing rooms, stagehands, and paychecks, and the world of the audience. If anyone ought to be aware of the arbitrariness of this barrier, it is the presenter, who must pay attention to both sides of the curtain at all times. Presenters, after all, must make certain that the show will go on. With them rests the ultimate responsibility for all phases of the performance: choosing artistic talent, providing technical backup, balancing budgets, raising money, promoting the event, and so on. In many cases, the presenter's job is thankless, and all the glory seems to go to the performers. But presenters have the unique opportunity to see both behind the curtain and in front—to observe the magic of the show and, at the same time, to be in on the secrets of that magic. Perhaps this is why so many of us, despite every kind of setback, complication, and disappointment, continue to find such satisfaction in presenting performances year after year.

Appendices

APPENDIX A — SAMPLE BYLAWS

BYLAWS OF MOLTO MUSIC AND DANCE SERIES, INC.

(A Massachusetts Nonprofit Corporation)

Section 1. NAME, PURPOSES, LOCATION, CORPORATE SEAL, AND FISCAL YEAR

1.1 Name and Purposes. The name and purposes of the corporation shall be set forth in the articles of incorporation.

1.2 Location. The principal office of the corporation in the Commonwealth of Massachusetts shall initially be located at the place set forth in the articles of incorporation of the corporation. The directors may change the location of the principal office in the Commonwealth of Massachusetts effective upon filing a certificate with the Secretary of the Commonwealth.

1.3 Corporate Seal. The directors may adopt and alter the seal of the corporation.

1.4 Fiscal Year. The fiscal year of the corporation shall, unless otherwise decided by the directors, end June 30 in each year.

Section 2. MEMBERS

The corporation shall have no members.

Section 3. SPONSORS, BENEFACTORS, CONTRIBUTORS, ADVISORS, FRIENDS OF THE CORPORATION

The directors may designate certain persons or groups of persons as sponsors, benefactors, contributors, advisers or friends of the corporation or such other title as they deem appropriate. Such persons shall serve in an honorary capacity and, except as the directors shall otherwise designate, shall in such capacity have no right to notice of or to vote at any meeting, shall not be considered for purposes of establishing a quorum, and shall have no other rights or responsibilities.

Section 4. BOARD OF DIRECTORS

4.1 Number, Election, and Tenure. The number of directors shall be twenty. At any special or regular meeting the directors then in office may increase the number of directors and elect new directors to complete the number so fixed; or they may decrease the number of directors but only to eliminate vacancies existing by reason of death, resignation, removal, or disqualification of one or more directors. Each director shall hold office for a fixed term of one, two, or three years as set by the other directors at the time of his election. If a director dies, resigns, is removed, becomes disqualified, or comes to the end of his term, his successor will be elected by a majority of directors then in office.

4.2 Powers. The affairs of the corporation shall be managed by the directors, who shall have and may exercise all the powers of the corporation.

4.3 Committees. The directors may elect or appoint one or more committees and may delegate to any such committee or committees any or all of their powers. Any committee to which the powers of the directors are delegated shall consist solely of directors. Unless the directors otherwise designate, committees shall conduct their affairs in the same manner as is provided in these bylaws for the directors. The members of any committee shall remain in office at the pleasure of the directors.

4.4 Suspension or Removal. A director may be suspended or removed with cause by vote of a majority of the directors then in office. A director may be removed with cause only after reasonable notice and opportunity to be heard.

4.5 Resignation. A director may resign by delivering his written resignation to the president, treasurer, or clerk of the corporation, to a meeting of directors or to the corporation at its principal office. Such resignation shall be effective upon receipt (unless specified to be effective at some other time) and acceptance thereof shall not be necessary to make it effective unless it so states.

4.6 Vacancies. Any vacancy in the board of directors, except a vacancy resulting from enlargement which must be filled in accordance with Section 4.1, may be filled by the directors. Each successor shall hold office for the unexpired term or until he sooner dies, resigns, is removed, or becomes disqualified. The directors shall have and may exercise all their powers notwithstanding the existence of one or more vacancies in their number.

4.7 Annual Meeting. The annual meeting of the directors shall be held at 12:00 o'clock noon on the fourth Friday in April in each year or if that date is a legal holiday in the place where the meeting is to be held, then at the same hour on the next succeeding day not a legal holiday. The annual meeting may be held at the principal office of the corporation or at such other place within the United States as the president or directors shall determine. Notice of any change of the date fixed in these bylaws for the annual meeting shall be given to all members at least twenty days before the new date fixed for such meeting.

4.8 Regular Meetings. Regular meetings of the directors may be held at such places and at such times as the directors may determine.

4.9 Special Meetings. Special meetings of the directors may be held at any time and at any place when called by the president or by two or more directors.

4.10 Call and Notice.

a. Regular Meetings. No call or notice shall be required for regular meetings of directors, provided that reasonable notice of the first regular meeting following the determination by the directors of the times and places for regular meetings shall be given to absent directors. Notice specifying the purpose of a regular meeting shall be given to each director if either contracts or transactions of the corporation with interested persons or amendments to these bylaws are to be considered at the meeting and shall be given as otherwise required by law, the articles of incorporation, or these bylaws.

b. Special Meetings. Reasonable notice of the time and place of special meetings of the directors shall be given to each director. Such notice need not specify the purposes of a meeting, unless otherwise required by law, the articles of incorporation, or these bylaws or unless there is to be considered at the meeting contracts or transactions of the corporation with interested persons, amendments to these bylaws, an increase or decrease in the number of directors, or removal or suspension of a director.

c. Reasonable and Sufficient Notice. Except as otherwise expressly provided, it shall be reasonable and sufficient notice to a director to send notice by mail at least forty-eight hours or by telegram at least twenty-four hours before the meeting addressed to him at his usual or last known business or residence address or to give notice to him in person or by telephone at least twenty-four hours before the meeting.

d. Waiver of Notice. Whenever notice of a meeting is required, such notice need not be given to any director if a written waiver of notice, executed by him (or his attorney thereunto authorized) before or after the meeting, is filed with the records of the meeting, or to any director who attends the meeting without protesting prior thereto or at its commencement the lack of notice to him. A waiver of notice need not specify the purposes of the meeting unless such purposes were required to be specified in the notice of such meeting.

4.11 Quorum. At any meeting of the directors a majority of the directors then in office shall constitute a quorum. Any meeting may be adjourned by a majority of the votes cast upon the question, whether or not a quorum is present, and the meeting may be held as adjourned without further notice.

4.12 Action by Vote. When a quorum is present at any meeting, a majority of the directors present and voting shall decide any question, including election of officers, unless otherwise provided by law, the articles of incorporation, or these bylaws.

4.13 Proxies. Members may vote either in person or by written proxy dated not more than six months before the meeting named therein, which proxies shall be filed before being voted with the clerk or other person responsible for recording the proceedings of the meeting. Unless otherwise specifically limited by their terms, such proxies shall entitle the holders thereof to vote at any adjournment of the meeting but the proxy shall terminate after the final adjournment of such meeting.

4.14 Action by Writing. Any action required or permitted to be taken at any meeting of the directors may be taken without a meeting if all the directors consent to the action in writing and the written consents are filed with the records of the meetings of the directors. Such consents shall be treated for all purposes as a vote of a meeting.

4.15 Compensation. Directors shall be precluded from receiving compensation for their services but shall be entitled to receive such amount, if any, as the directors may from time to time determine, to cover expenses of attendance at meetings.

Section 5. OFFICERS AND AGENTS

5.1 Number and Qualification. The officers of the corporation shall be a president, treasurer, clerk, and such other officers, if any, as the directors may determine. The corporation may also have such agents, if any, as the directors may appoint. An officer may but need not be a director. The clerk shall be a resident of Massachusetts unless the corporation has a resident agent duly appointed for the purpose of service of process. A person may hold more than one office at the same time. If required by the directors, any officer shall give the corporation a bond for the faithful performance of his duties in such amount and with such surety or sureties as shall be satisfactory to the directors.

5.2 Election. The president, treasurer, and clerk shall be elected annually by the directors at their first meeting. Other officers, if any, may be elected by the directors at any time.

5.3 Tenure. The president, treasurer, and clerk shall be elected at the annual meeting and shall hold office until their successors are chosen.

5.4 President. The president shall be the chief executive officer of the corporation and, subject to the control of the directors, shall have general charge and supervision of the affairs of the corporation. The president shall preside at all meetings of the directors, except as the directors otherwise determine.

5.5 Treasurer. The treasurer shall be the chief financial officer and the chief accounting officer of the corporation. He shall be in charge of its financial affairs, funds, securities, and valuable papers and shall keep full and accurate records thereof. He shall have such other duties and powers as designated by the directors or the president. He shall also be in charge of its books of account and accounting records, and of its accounting procedures.

5.6 Clerk. The clerk shall record and maintain records of all proceedings of the directors in a book or series of books kept for that purpose, which book or books shall be kept within the Commonwealth at the principal office of the corporation or at the office of its clerk or of its resident agent and shall be open at all reasonable times to the inspection of any person. Such book or books shall also contain records of all meetings of the incorporator and the original, or attested copies, of the articles of organization and bylaws and names of all directors and the address of each. If the clerk is absent from any meeting of members or directors, a temporary clerk chosen at the meeting shall exercise the duties of the clerk at the meeting.

5.7 Suspension or Removal. An officer may be suspended or removed with or without cause by vote of majority of directors then in office at any special meeting called for such purpose or at any regular meeting. An officer may be removed with cause only after reasonable notice and opportunity to be heard.

5.8 Resignation. An officer may resign by delivering his written resignation to the president, treasurer, or clerk of the corporation, to a meeting of the directors, or to the corporation at its principal office. Such resignation shall be effective upon receipt (unless specified to be effective at some other time), and acceptance thereof shall not be necessary to make it effective unless it so states.

5.9 Vacancies. If the office of any officer becomes vacant, the directors may elect a successor. Each such successor shall hold office for the unexpired term, and in the case of the president, treasurer, and clerk until his successor is elected and qualified, or in each case until he sooner dies, resigns, is removed, or becomes disqualified.

Section 6. EXECUTION OF PAPERS

Except as the directors may generally or in particular cases authorize the execution thereof in some other manner, all deeds, leases, transfers, contracts, bonds, notes, checks, drafts and other obligations made, accepted, or endorsed by the corporation shall be signed by the president or by the treasurer.

Any recordable instrument purporting to affect an interest in real estate, executed in the name of the corporation by two of its officers, of whom one is the president and the other is the treasurer, shall be binding on the corporation in favor of a purchaser or other person relying in good faith on such instrument notwithstanding any inconsistent provisions of the articles of incorporation, bylaws, resolutions, or votes of the corporation.

Section 7. PERSONAL LIABILITY

The directors and officers of the corporation shall not be personally liable for any debt, liability, or obligation of the corporation. All persons, corporations, or other entities extending credit to, contracting with, or having any claim against, the corporation, may look only to the funds and property of the corporation for the payment of any such contract or claim, or for the payment of any debt, damages, judgment, or decree, or of any money that may otherwise become due or payable to them from the corporation.

Section 8. AMENDMENTS

These bylaws may be altered, amended, or repealed in whole or in part by vote of a majority of the directors then in office.

Section 9. PROCEDURE

Robert's Rules of Order shall govern the meetings of the board of directors in all matters not provided for in these bylaws.

APPENDIX B — SAMPLE CONTRACT AND RIDERS

SAMPLE CONTRACT

(Name and address of booking agent goes here with phone number.)

AGREEMENT, as follows, made this .... day of .... 19..... by and between .... herein called 'Artist,' contracting through .... herein called 'Artist's Manager' and .... herein called 'Presenter' whose address is

____

____

1. The Presenter hereby engages and the Artist and the Artist's Manager agree hereby to perform the engagement hereinafter provided, upon all of the terms and conditions herein set forth.

A. ENGAGEMENT INFORMATION

Date(s)	Time	Hall/Location/City
__________	______	____________
__________	______	____________
__________	______	____________

B. REHEARSAL INFORMATION

__________	______	____________
__________	______	____________

2. Presenter agrees to furnish at its own expense a suitable theater, hall, or auditorium in said city, on the date and at the time for the performance(s) above mentioned, well heated, lighted, clean, and in good order, with a clean, comfortable dressing room near the stage for Artist, and to pay for taking show in and out and working same (if consisting of a company or troupe), furnishing all electricians and stage hands required, also to pay for all lights, tickets, house programs, license (if required), heating, cleaning, services of all necessary at-

taches, special police, ushers, ticket sellers for advance, or single sales (whether such sales take place in the theater or elsewhere), ticket-takers, bill-posting, mailing and distributing of circulars and daily display newspaper advertising in the principal newspapers, and all other necessary expenses in connection therewith. NO SEATS WILL BE PERMITTED ON THE STAGE WITHOUT THE CONSENT OF ARTIST.

3. Presenter represents that it has a lease for the theater, hall, or auditorium, covering the date or dates of this engagement, which lease will be shown to Artist or Artist's Manager upon request.

4. Presenter agrees to furnish, without charge, properly tuned, one grand piano for use at the above concert unless Artist is able to and does obtain pianos without expense, through affiliations with piano makers or dealers, and so advises Presenter.

5. Artist agrees to supply the usual quantity of printing and advertising material as available, and will also furnish copy of the program which is to be printed and distributed by the Presenter. Presenter hereby agrees to print said copy in its entirety.

6. In the event that Presenter refuses or neglects to provide any of the items hereinbefore stated, Artist shall have the right to refuse to perform this contract, and the Presenter shall be liable to Artist for any damages on account thereof.

7. Not later than the first intermission of the first performance, or immediately before the performance if there is to be no intermission, Presenter will deliver to .... the sum of .... in lawful United States funds, or by check payable to the order of ....
In the event that payments are not made as herein provided, Artist shall, at his or her option, have the right to refuse to continue the performance and Presenter shall remain liable to Artist for the agreed price herein set forth, unless other arrangements for payment are explicitly set forth in riders to this contract.

8. If before the date of any scheduled concert, Artist or Artist's Manager finds that Presenter has failed, neglected or refused to perform any contract with another artist for an earlier concert engagement, or if Artist or Artist's Manager finds that the financial credit of Presenter has been impaired, Artist shall have the right to cancel this contract.

9. The Artist shall be under no liability for failure to appear or perform in the event that such failure is caused by or due to the physical disability of Artist, or acts or regulations of public authorities, labor difficulties, civil tumult, strike, epidemic, interruption or delay of transportation service, or any other cause beyond the control of Artist.

10. This contract cannot be assigned or transferred without the written consent of Artist's Manager, and contains the complete understanding of the parties respecting the subject matter hereof. It is not binding upon Artist until executed and delivered by the office of Artist's Manager and Artist's Manager signs only as Artist's agent and is not obligated hereunder and is not responsible for any acts or defaults of Artist.

11. No radio apparatus or transmitting device shall be used during the concert or concerts in any manner or form, in the building in which the concert or concerts shall be given, without the written consent of Artist or Artist's Manager.

12. This contract includes rider(s). The contract is not binding until all riders have been initialled by Presenter and Artist or Artist's Manager.

ARTIST ....

BY ....

PRESENTER ....

BY ....

Failure to supply the following information may seriously interfere with the proper fulfillment of the contract by the Artist:

ATTRACTION ....

DATE ....

CITY ....

NAME OF HALL ....

HOUR OF CONCERT ....

HOUR OF REHEARSAL ....

BEST HOTEL (if hospitality not provided) ....

NAME AND ADDRESS OF PERSON MAKING CONTRACT ....

....

PARTY TO BE NOTIFIED ON ARRIVAL, ADDRESS AND TELEPHONE NUMBER,

SPECIAL INFORMATION ....

....

....

SAMPLE RIDERS

RIDER A

service #..........................place............................ in the city of ....

on .... 19...... at............................ o'clock in the ....

service #..........................place............................ in the city of ....

on .... 19...... at............................ o'clock in the ....

RIDER B*

The touring staff of the Artist Company consists of a Company Manager, a Rehearsal Supervisor, a Production Stage Manager, an Assistant Stage Manager, and a Wardrobe Supervisor. We carry our own costumes, sets, props, and color (gel) for lighting. We require the presenter to provide lighting equipment, soft goods, crew, adequate stage surface for bare-footed dancing, sound system, and dressing room facilities as noted below.

The figures below represent the Company's maximum requirement. Based upon the number of programs presented, the choice of repertory, and the amount of work that can be accomplished prior to the Company's arrival at the theater, these requirements can oftentimes be reduced.

LIGHTING EQUIPMENT

Instruments:

- 20 8" Lekos or equivalent in front of house coves or box boom positions
- 90 to 120 6" Lekos (6x9 ERS and 6x12 ERS depending upon batten trims; 6" Kliegel Lekos are not acceptable)
- 25 to 35 8" fresnels
- 15 to 20 8' R40 strip sections, 3 circuits per section, 300 w

Hardware:

- 8 10' booms with 50 lb. bases for mounting lights
- 32 12" sidearms with single "T"

Controls:

- 60 patchable dimmers
  - 48 at minimum rating of 3 kw per dimmer
  - 12 at minimum rating of 6 kw per dimmer

Cable:

- enough to circuit light plot as submitted by Company Stage Manager 4-6 weeks prior to arrival

SOUND

- Two 7 1/2 ips 1/4-inch reel-to-reel tape decks
- Mixer with a minimum of 4 channels
- 2 two-channel amplifiers
- 2 speakers of sufficient quality to fill the Hall
- 2 backstage monitors
- Microphone
- Headset communications between stage manager's position and running crew

SOFT GOODS

- 5 sets of black legs prehung to form four 6' wing openings
- 5 black borders
- full stage black drop hung upstage leaving at least a 4' crossover
- full stage white or light blue cyclorama (or scrim and bounce) hung upstage

FLOOR

- Stage floor should be clean and free of nails, splinters, or any other protrusions
- A linoleum or Marley-type vinyl floor is a highly preferable surface and, depending upon floor conditions, may be required
- *Please note that dancers cannot be penalized for refusal to rehearse or perform on a concrete floor even though it is covered with linoleum or wood laid directly on the concrete.*

DRESSING ROOMS

- Should have ample tables, mirrors, and make-up lights for 9 women and 9 men
- An extra room near the dressing rooms for wardrobe equipped with an iron and an ironing board
- *nonpublic* lavatory facilities
- Ice should be readily available at all rehearsals and performances.

CREW

If theater is a union house:

- For load-in and load-out
  - 8 to 10 electricians
  - 5 to 7 carpenters

- 1 to 3 prop men

- For rehearsal and performance
  - 6 to 8 electricians
  - 5 to 7 carpenters
  - 2 to 6 prop men
  - 1 to 2 wardrobe personnel for each rehearsal, performance and load out

If theater is a nonunion house:

- 10 to 12 *skilled* technicians for load-in, run of show, and load-out

PLEASE NOTE: The crew for *all* rehearsals and performances must be the same people. *No exceptions.*

TIME NEEDED IN THEATER

Maximum call (dependent upon stage and crew conditions and programming):

- 8 hours day *before* first performance
- 8 hours (including special rehearsal) + show call day of performance

If a second program is requested:

- 4 hours minimum + spacing rehearsal for each change of program

PLEASE NOTE: Dancers must have access to stage two hours before curtain time.

MINI-CONCERT

- Possible in performance theater only
- May be scheduled only upon completion of performance load-in and spacing rehearsal
- All technical requirements above as for performance

**Rider B* is adapted from a rider provided courtesy of The Paul Taylor Dance Company and is included as a sample rider only, not as an indication of the company's current technical requirements.

APPENDIX C — SAMPLE PRESS RELEASE

From: Molto Music Series
Centerville, Massachusetts 01001

FOR IMMEDIATE RELEASE

Contact: John Smith, Publicity director
617-777-0101

October 15, 1991

ROMA CHAMBER PLAYERS MAKE TRIUMPHANT RETURN TO MOLTO MUSIC SERIES
PROGRAM TO INCLUDE BEETHOVEN'S *GHOST* TRIO

The nationally acclaimed Roma Chamber Players will return to the Centerville Opera House next Saturday, October 30, after a triumphant tour of North America. Tickets for the 8:15 concert are now available at the Centerville Book Store.

In recognition of the Centerville audience's overwhelming response to selections performed in Roma's concert last year, this year's program will include Beethoven's *Ghost* trio.

George Smith, artistic director of the Roma Chamber Players, has promised an exciting evening of music, saying "the *Ghost* is a particularly apt inclusion given the concert date. We believe it will serve as an appropriately electrifying welcome to Halloween."

Susan Cook, a violinist in the group, explains that Beethoven has proven to be an audience favorite in Roma's Centerville performances. "When we played Beethoven's *Archduke* trio last year, the Centerville audience gave us a standing ovation," she says. "The concert committee has asked us to program another Beethoven trio for this concert and the *Ghost* is one of our favorites."

Since last year, the Roma Chamber Players have been heard in major cities across North America including New York, Boston, Toronto, and Los Angeles. Critical acclaim has followed the musicians wherever they have played. Said Michael Rineberg of the *Boston News*: "Over and above the fact that they are technically proficient, the group's musicianship is impeccable. It is a pleasure simply to sit back and listen."

Centerville audiences have been vocal in their appreciation of Roma's artistic abilities, says Joanne Baker, President of Molto Music Series. "We have received more favorable comments about their performance last year than on practically any event in our history," she says. "We feel fortunate that the Roma Chamber Players could fit us into their busy schedule again this year."

Tickets for the 8:15 concert are on sale now at the Centerville Book Store for $8 and $12; the low ticket prices have been made possible by funding support from the National Endowment for the Arts and the State Council on the Arts and Humanities. In addition, students and senior citizens may purchase tickets at a special $4 price, thanks to a grant from the Beller Foundation. Tickets also will be available at the door beginning at 7:30 p.m. the night of the concert.

APPENDIX D — SAMPLE FUND-RAISING LETTER

Dear Friends:

With Molto Music's eleventh season successfully completed, it is time to take stock and to prepare for our annual metamorphosis. Next year, our program will be substantially different once again. As usual, there will be new faces on stage, new music, and new productions. Just as in each of the previous seasons, the coming one promises new growth and maturity.

As we look back, we can be proud of this season's accomplishments. The new auditorium, to which we moved with some apprehension, was filled with standing-room-only audiences for most events. Our budget increased by more than 15 percent, thanks partly to a generous grant from the Beller Foundation and also to continuing support from our loyal contributors. Our school program continued to delight children of all ages. During the past year, 421 kids danced, sang, and clowned with 15 professional performers.

And what is promised for next season? We will present our first mime show, with a week of mime workshops in the schools; we will initiate a reduced-price ticket program for senior citizens; and we will make substantial improvements in the auditorium's lighting system. Our plans promise growth not only in size but in quality.

It is crucial to our organization's continuing vitality that we continue to develop as we have in the past. It is the help of our friends that has made such growth possible. That help is made up of interest, enthusiasm, patience, moral support, and money. We are aware of the abundance of intangibles you have given us, and we shall always welcome them. Can you also celebrate the end of another wonderful season by sending a tax-deductible contribution that will help next year off to a flying start?

Sincerely,

Judith Grey
Artistic Director

Virginia Carey
President of the Board

APPENDIX E — PROCEDURE FOR APPLYING TO THE NATIONAL ENDOWMENT FOR THE ARTS

1. Review the *Guide to Programs* (available from NEA, Washington, D.C., 20506).

2. Write and request printed guidelines for the specific program(s) in which you are interested.

3. When you receive the guidelines, review them VERY carefully. Does your organization meet preliminary eligibility requirements? Are the programmatic elements and priorities for support expressed in the guidelines consistent with your organization's goals? Can you match the federal dollar at least one for one?

4. BEFORE FILLING OUT AND SUBMITTING AN OFFICIAL APPLICATION:

   a. Invest a few dollars and call the Program Office at the Endowment (number will be in the guidelines booklet). Ask for the "Program Specialist" in charge of applications submitted under your specific category in the guidelines.

   b. Introduce yourself to the Program Specialist, indicate that you have read the guidelines and are interested in applying, and that you would like to discuss the project and application procedures.

   c. Describe your project and its relevance to the guidelines. You will probably be asked questions on organizational structure, project budget, matching funds, and personnel. The Program Specialist may advise you immediately if the project is acceptable under program guidelines and, if so, will suggest that you submit a formal application. You should not take this to mean that the project will be funded.

   Program Specialists are your most valuable contact at the Endowment. They are trained to answer your questions on almost every topic, or to know where to find the answers. They are on your side, so be pleasant and personable in your approach to them. Not only are they generally experts in their own right, with substantial artistic or administrative credentials, but they have to respond daily to a national constituency and are overworked. Do not be frivolous or demanding upon their time. If you can, plan to meet

Program Specialists in person if you should be going to Washington or if both of you happen to be attending a national or regional arts conference.

d. If you are told that the project is not appropriate to the guidelines, ask if there are other programs at the Endowment under which you might apply. If you are referred to another program, repeat all the steps under "4" above.

5. Call your NEA Regional Representative (your state arts agency can provide you with this person's name, address, and phone number). Arrange for a site visit if possible but at least discuss your application in detail. Also call your state arts agency and alert the staff that you will be submitting an application to the Endowment. Ask for help and advice and, perhaps, a letter of support.

6. Before you fill out the application, carefully read the application form instructions. If there is something you do not understand, call the Program Specialist. If your description of the project does not fit into the space provided, it is too long. Include all required supplementary materials specified in the guidelines. Type the application—do not submit a handwritten one. Do not forget to sign and date it. The application should be shipped certified mail by the postmark date. Late applications are generally not accepted.

7. Applications are reviewed first by a panel of advisers who make recommendations to the National Council on the Arts. The Council reviews the panel recommendations and makes its own recommendations to the Chair of NEA. This whole process (from application submission to grant letter) takes slightly less than a year; and, generally, it is not advisable to try to find out what the recommendation of the panel or Council has been on your application. Specific questions about the procedure and the timing can be answered by Program Specialists, but do not badger them for information which they cannot provide.

8. Generally speaking, no news is good news. Rejections are sent out immediately at various stages of the review process. Grant award letters are often delayed several months past the final decision date. Since most applications are funded at a level that is less than the requested amount, a "Revised Budget" form will generally precede a grant letter. You must fill out, sign, and return it prior to a grant letter being processed.

APPENDIX F[1] — WHAT DOES IT MEAN? *A Glossary of Terms*

This is not a standard glossary in alphabetical order. It has been broken down into categories, and items have been addressed more or less in their order of importance. This glossary really presents a discussion of the elements of production and a look at some potential problems.

The first section deals with stage directions and terminology for basic technological communication. The second section addresses stage rigging and fly systems. The third section deals with masking and draperies. The fourth section describes the instrument-mounting positions. The final section describes stage electrical equipment in some depth.

STAGE DIRECTIONS

Directions. In the theater, lateral directions are given in terms of *stage left* and *stage right.* This is the performer's left and right as he or she faces the audience and is the orientation used by technicians. *Upstage* and *downstage* are terms that originated in the time of raked stages, when the back of the stage floor was slanted higher than the front. Thus the portion of the stage closest to the audience is downstage, and the back of the stage is upstage. *House left* and *house right* are terms used by box office and house staffs, and refer to the right/left orientation of the audience member facing the stage.

Proscenium Arch. The proscenium arch is the opening in the downstage wall separating the audience from the stage. In older theaters the proscenium is usually a true architectural arch, often highly decorated. More recent architectural practice has been to minimize the proscenium to the point where the actual arch may be simple movable panels or only draperies.

[1] This glossary has been reprinted by permission of Western States Arts Federation (WESTAF) from its *Technical Production Handbook* by M. K. Barrell. Copies of the *Technical Production Handbook* may be ordered from Judy Hertzl, WESTAF, 236 Montezuma Ave., Santa Fe, NM 87501.

Fly Loft. The fly loft (or *fly gallery*) is the space directly above the stage area where draperies and lighting instruments are hung. Ideally, the height of the fly loft is three times as high as the proscenium arch to allow for the scenic elements to be flown out of sight. From the outside of the building, the fly loft is that huge rectangular block of masonry that identifies most theaters in the world as theaters. For either economic or aesthetic reasons, many people who build theaters—but never have to use them—see fit to reduce the size of the fly loft or to eliminate it entirely. For most forms of production, this is a grave omission. If your theater claims to be a proscenium theater but has a height-to-proscenium ratio of less than three to one, be sure to let a prospective company know, because it can greatly inhibit their ability to produce properly.

Grid. The grid is the metal framework at the top of the fly loft or just below the stage roof. Consider it as the ceiling of the fly loft. Everything that hangs or flies on the stage is suspended from the grid. When a company asks about the height of the grid, they usually want to know how far out (or how high) the battens (see below) fly.

Dead-Hung. Many theaters do not have a fly loft or the ability to fly equipment and scenery in and out. Instead of a grid, there are nonmovable—or dead-hung—pipes. To hang or remove instruments, you must climb up to the pipes, rather than bringing them to the deck or stage as with a fly system.

Stage or Deck. The stage or deck is the entire floor of the theater inside the stage house under the grid. The term *on stage* denotes that area of the stage that is visible to the audience. The term *off stage* denotes that area hidden from the view of the audience.

Apron. The apron of a stage is that area of the floor that extends through the proscenium arch toward the audience.

Wing. The wing is the area off stage hidden from the view of the audience by masking. A wing is a space, not a drapery.

Plaster Line. The plaster line is the primary reference point for determining measurements up and down stage. It is a line drawn across the stage at the upstage edge of the proscenium. For instance, if the upstage corner of the set is listed on the paperwork as being thirty-three feet six inches, it means that the corner is thirty-three feet six inches upstage of the plaster line. The plaster line is the determiner of the downstage limit of the stage separating the stage from the apron.

Curtain Line. The curtain line is a term similar to the plaster line, in that it is a reference point for measuring up and down stage. It is less accurate a measurement than the plaster line, however, because the act curtain can measure anywhere from one foot to two feet wide at the bottom, and heating and air conditioning can make it shift as much as four feet. The plaster line is the preferred measurement.

Center Line. The center line is the major reference line for measuring laterally on stage. It is the line running directly down the middle of the stage, separating stage left from stage right. All measurements on the stage are made up and down from the plaster line and left and right from the center line.

Ground Plan. The ground plan (often called just a *plan*) is an aerial view of the stage drawn to a specific scale (usually one-quarter inch equals one foot or one-half inch equals one foot), showing all the pertinent elements of the stage. It is a prime tool of theater technicians for planning productions and for communicating stage information with one another. Every theater should have an accurate ground plan, which should be included in any technical communications. (Do not use the architect's plans that were used to build the building. These lack the proper information needed by technicians. "As built" and "as designed" are often two different things.)

Section. A section is a side view of the stage as seen through the middle of the stage. This drawing, though not required, can be very valuable for larger, more complex facilities. Its primary value is to allow a designer or technician to see if the show will *mask*. To mask a show is to hide all extraneous elements from the audience using a combination of the scenic elements, legs, and borders.

Light Plot. A light plot is a plan view of the stage with the lighting instruments superimposed, showing where each is hung, what type it is, what dimmer it is patched into, what circuit it is plugged into, and what color it is gelled. Some light plots are drawn directly over a ground plan of the stage; some are drawn in a schematic style and not necessarily done to the scale of the stage. The light plot is provided by the company's lighting designer to the presenter.

Hanger Log. A hanger log (often called a *hanging schedule* or *hanger sheet*) is a document describing the location of each line set in a rigging system (see below). This is a critical document. The presenter generates the base hanger log. It shows not only the number of line sets (see below), but the distance upstage from the plaster line, and any specifics impacting the use of those lines, for example, how long the battens are, how far out the battens fly, what items are permanently hung on which battens, and what is traditionally hung on battens to best mask the house (lines usually reserved for legs and borders). Any oddity of the fly system should be stated here, such as lines that will not fly all the way out, bent battens, or clearance problems.

In listing battens that cannot be stripped, you need to remember that there is a difference between items that cannot be moved and items that are inconvenient to move or remove. Some technicians never like to take their lighting instruments or draperies off the pipes. For some small touring companies traveling without any equipment or scenery this may not be an inconvenience, but for a large production carrying its own lighting and scenery it can be cause for cancellation of a contract. If a company's tech rider requires a stripped house before load-in, they mean it. In a situation like this the safest place for your drapes and lighting instruments is off the stage and in storage.

Once the company receives the hanger log from the presenter, the company's technical director will fill out the company's requirements in the log and return it to the presenter. This gives the presenter's technical director an indication of what will be moving into the theater. It is this technical director's responsibility to read the completed log and react to any potential problems.

Because it is impossible to fly the battens in a dead-hung house, it is all the more important to find a creative way to describe what is available and possible to do in your theater. An accurate diagram of the battens or grid-work is usually a helpful tool. As the height of the battens cannot be changed, it is crucial to know exactly what that height is. With a dead-hung stage, factors that one tends to take for granted on a traditional stage—the diameter and weight of the pipes themselves or the breaking strength of the chain, cable, rope, or pipe clamps supporting those pipes—become very important. Some dead-hung houses are well engineered and well designed; some are not and may actually present a safety hazard. A full electric batten or a large velour drape can weigh more than one thousand pounds. If the battens are hung with a simple dog chain (as many of them are), they are completely unsafe and should not be used. Many dead-hung houses do not even have battens for the draperies, but useless lightweight aluminum tracks.

STAGE RIGGING AND FLY SYSTEMS

Stage rigging is a misunderstood and potentially dangerous form of machinery. All presenters need to know at least a little about that tangle of rope and cable dangling over their heads.

Systems. The *rigging* or *fly system* is a series of cables, pulleys, and counterweight-filled arbors that enable scenery, drapes, or lighting equipment to *fly* in and out. This ability to make scenery change almost instantly is what helps create the "magic of theater." There are three basic types of fly systems. *Hemp or Sandbag:* The hemp or sandbag system is the oldest and, these days, the rarest of the available types of rigging. It uses hemp ropes to support the battens and the scenic elements attached to them. The batten is counterbalanced by several large sandbags. This is an old system but can work well in the hands of a competent *flyman* (who is rarer than the system). Many modern theaters use a few sandbag lines to augment their regular systems. *Synchronous Winch:* The second, newest style of rigging system uses synchronous winches to lift the battens. This approach has worked with mixed results in a limited number of theaters around the country. The idea has merit, but the winches have myriad inherent problems, and few installations work flawlessly the way a rigging system needs to work. *Counterweight:* The most common rigging system is called the counterweight system. The battens are supported by metal aircraft cable, and the counterbalances are steel or iron counterweights held in a large metal arbor. Because this is the system used in 95 percent of all theaters, it is explored in more depth below.

Line Set. The line set describes a single working group of elements that enables scenery or lighting equipment to move up and down or to fly. A pipe is attached by cables and pulleys to a counterweight arbor placed against the stage wall. When the arbor is pulled toward the stage, the pipe (or batten) moves toward the grid or *flies out.* When the arbor is pulled toward the grid, the pipe (or batten) moves toward the stage floor or *flies in.* A group of line sets creates a fly system. For a moderately large theater, 50 to 60 line sets is common, although some stages get up to the range of 100-120. Line sets are usually evenly spaced up and down stage on six-, eight- or nine-inch centers.

Batten. A batten is a horizontal steel pipe attached to the cables of the fly system. All scenery and lighting equipment are tied or clamped to the battens. Preferably a batten will be approximately twenty feet longer than the width of the proscenium (a forty-foot proscenium would have sixty-foot battens). Battens were originally made of wood and adapted from battens on sailing ships. In fact, a major portion of theatrical rigging design and terminology comes directly from the rigging of sailing ships.

Lift Lines. The lift lines are the steel aircraft cables that support the batten. Each line set will use anywhere from three to nine lift lines, depending on the size of the batten. The lift lines then run to the grid and are supported by the sheaves in the loftblocks and the headblocks.

Sheave. The sheave (pronounced "shiv") is actually the pulley portion of a *loftblock* or *headblock*, but in common use it is the term that describes loftblocks and headblocks.

Loftblock. A loftblock is the single-sheave unit mounted on the grid as a support for each single lift line run.

Headblock. A headblock is the group of three to nine sheaves mounted together as a single unit in which all the lift lines from a single batten come together. The headblock is mounted to a steel beam (called the *headblock beam*) at the side wall of the stage house above the area where the line sets are operated.

Floorblock. A floorblock or tension block is a single block mounted on the stage floor (or sometimes below stage level) that redirects the endless line back toward the headblock on the grid.

Arbor. After the lift lines go over the loftblock and the headblock they head down the stagehouse wall and are attached to an arbor. The arbor is a rectangular steel carriage designed to hold counterweights. Depending on the size of the theater, an arbor will be from five to twelve feet long, and hold from 600 to 2,000 pounds of steel counterweights. It is guided in its travel up and down the stagehouse wall by either *Tee-track guides* or *wire-guides*.

Tee-track. Tee-track is a steel latticework of parallel bars used to guide and control the arbor. This is the preferred type of arbor guide for all medium and large theaters.

Wire-guide. Wire-guides are parallel aircraft cables running through holes on the edges of the arbor and stretched between the grid and the stage. Compared with tee-track, they are a much cheaper, less efficient, and more dangerous form of guiding the arbor travel. This system is acceptable in small theaters with few line sets and low grid height.

Endless Line. Attached at the bottom of each arbor there is a rope, usually 5/8-inch to 3/4-inch manila hemp. This is the actual rope that is pulled by the operator (called a *flyman*) that makes the system work. The endless line (often called the *rope, purchase line,* or *line*) runs from the bottom of the arbor to the stage deck where it runs around another sheave on a floorblock or tension block. The endless line then runs directly back up to the grid, over the same headblock that supports the lift lines, and down to the arbor where it is attached at the top of the arbor. This is why it is called an endless line: it becomes a circle of rope with the arbor attached in the middle. Therefore, when the flyman pulls on the back side of the endless line (the one attached to the bottom of the arbor and farthest away from the operator), the arbor flies (travels) in (toward the stage) and the batten flies out (toward the grid). When the flyman pulls on the front side of the endless line, the arbor flies out and the batten flies in.

Simple and effective, yes, but very dangerous. Thousands of pounds of weight are moving in and out above the performers' heads. As productions change, the weights have to change, and the potential for battens and arbors getting out of control is enormous. A line set flies smoothly only as long as the arbor is correctly counterweighted. If an arbor is "out of weight" it can be a deadly missile.

Locking Rail and Rope Lock. The endless line passes through a locking mechanism called a *rope lock*, which is mounted on a steel bar called a *locking rail*. The locking rail is mounted sometimes on the stage floor and sometimes on a *pinrail,* or working platform, built several feet above the stage floor to preserve stage space or allow for openings in the wall for doors or alcoves. This is the place where the flyman operates the system.

Loading Platform. A platform or catwalk built near the grid in front of the arbors is called a loading platform or *loading dock*. It is the position from which the arbors are loaded or counterweighted.

Single Purchase/Double Purchase. There are two variations of the counterweight rigging system that are quite different in their impact on a production. The system described above is called a single-purchase system. This means that there is a one-to-one mechanical ratio with the endless line. The batten travels one foot for each foot that the arbor travels.

The double-purchase system adds a second sheave at the bottom of the arbor where the endless line travels through and back down to the floorblock. With this system the batten travels two feet for every one foot that the arbor travels, because the added sheave gives an added mechanical advantage (double purchase). This system allows the floorblock to be mounted on the pintail rather than on the stage floor, thus freeing up the lower portion of the stage wall for doors, alcoves, storage, or whatever. This style has many advantages on paper for architects looking for space or gimmicks. To anyone who has ever actually worked a show from a pintail it is a disaster. The two-to-one mechanical advantage becomes a two-to-one weight disadvantage. This means that if a large scenic wall weighs 900 pounds, the weight loader must add 1,800 pounds of counterweight. This is an extremely slow process and opens the door for even more danger of a poorly loaded arbor. There is an incredible amount of added inertia in a double-purchase system, making the process of getting the arbor moving and, more importantly, getting it stopped extremely difficult. The rope also travels twice as far in a double-purchase system, making any pull of a rope twice as long for the flyman.

With many productions the quality of the fly system is not a factor, but when a large show with many scenic elements moves into your facility and the company must make that show work with little or no rehearsal, the quality of the fly system can become the single most important element of your theater. If you ever have a chance to be involved in the construction or renovation of a theater, please fight for a single-purchase system. Many theaters get a reputation of having an inept and slow fly crew. Before the crew is accused, the rigging system should be examined; with a double-purchase system, the best flyman in the world can look like a fool.

Trim. The distance between the deck and a batten indicating the height of that batten when it is in a working position is called the *trim height.*

MASKING AND DRAPERIES

Any drapery or scenic piece used to define the stage or impede the view of the audience is called *masking.* Masking terminology is an area with a great deal of duplication and incorrect application of terms.

Border. A border is a horizontal drape used to control the area of the stage seen by the audience and to hide from view items in the fly loft, such as lighting equipment and scenery.

Leg. A leg is a vertical masking piece hung at the sides of the stage used to hide the wing spaces and define the width of the stage. A series of legs and borders is the most common form of masking for dance.

Wing. The wing is the offstage space between the legs.

Grand Drape. The grand drape is the first (downstage) border. In older theaters, it is often highly ornamental. It is the visual determiner of the height of the proscenium opening (called the *trim height*). It is not the main curtain that opens and closes.

Tormentor or Torm. The tormentor is the first (downstage) leg. It can be a soft drapery but is often framed and solid. This is the first visual determiner of the width of the stage.

Teaser. The term *teaser* is used to define the first horizontal masking piece. Used in conjunction with a tormentor, this first masking set of the tormentor and teaser becomes what is often called a *portal.* What is really a grand drape and what is a teaser is a gray area. In rigid definition, the tormentor and the teaser are the first framed masking pieces used as a set to form a portal. Occasionally a theater will have both a grand drape and a teaser. Not all horizontal masking pieces are teasers; only the first piece is a teaser (the rest are borders), unless it is a grand drape. See how simple!

Act Curtain or House Curtain. The act curtain is the curtain that opens and closes, separating the audience from the stage. It is usually hung directly upstage of the grand drape. It can either open in the center (called *traveling*), or it can fly in and out (called *guillotining*).

Asbestos or Fire Curtain. A fire-resistant curtain located at the proscenium opening immediately downstage of the act curtain, the fire curtain is required by law for most stages. Because asbestos is now illegal, it has been replaced by fiberglass woven fabrics. The most common brand name is Zee-tex. Often a small border of asbestos (Zee-tex) is hung on an *electric* (see below) to keep lighting instruments from burning draperies.

Cyclorama. A cyclorama (usually called just a *cyc*) is a large fabric drop rigged at the back of the stage, with curved arms wrapping downstage enclosing the stage. It was designed to create sky effects and to give a feeling of great depth. A true wraparound cyc is usually not applicable for a dance production because the downstage curved portion provides a barrier that makes exits and side-lighting difficult or impossible.

Sky Drop. A sky drop is a flat fabric drop at the back of the stage used for sky effects without wrapping downstage like a cyclorama. It is sometimes referred to as a *cyc*.

Scrim. A scrim is a transparent gauze material used for stage effects such as ghosts, clouds, or any effect requiring something to appear and disappear. When lit from the front, it becomes opaque. When lit from the back, it becomes transparent. A scrim is often used in front of a skydrop to give more sense of depth. The most common fabric for a scrim is called *sharkstooth*; other fabrics are *opera net* and *bobinette*.

INSTRUMENT-MOUNTING POSITIONS

Any dimmable lighting fixture on the stage is called a *lighting instrument*. The lighting instruments are clamped to a pipe. This pipe is then called an *electrical mounting position*. Any pipe anywhere can be a mounting position for temporary situations, but the term mounting position refers to a pipe specifically mounted for hanging lighting instruments. This pipe will usually have an electrical raceway called a *connector strip* bolted to or adjacent to it, with multiple dimmable circuits inside the strip. Some mounting positions are permanent, whereas others are portable. Mounting positions, especially those in the front of house, can change from theater to theater. This variation in mounting positions can make the job of lighting a touring show in a short time very tricky.

Electric. An electric (or *electric batten*) is an on-stage batten with cable and connectors mounted on it, specifically used for hanging instruments. The electric can fly in and out with the other battens in the fly system. Electrics can be parallel to the proscenium like most of the fly system, or they can be perpendicular to the proscenium, mounted at the sides of the stage. These are called side electrics and are most often used for dance. The term *electric* is also used in dead-hung houses.

Bridge. Bridge is the term used for an electric constructed from a large truss-work instead of the simple batten. The bridge was originally designed so that a stagehand could move about on it to adjust the carbons of early carbon-arc spotlights.

Boom. A boom is a vertical pipe used for mounting lighting instruments. On-stage booms are usually portable. The terms *tree, tower,* and *ladder* are often used as variations for a portable boom. When mounted in the auditorium, booms are usually a permanent fixture. *House booms* are permanent booms mounted to the auditorium wall. *Box booms* are mounted in or on a box seat. *Balcony booms* are mounted in the balcony.

F.O.H. (Front of House). Front of house refers to any mounting position in the auditorium. *A.P. (Ante-Pro)* refers to a mounting position in the auditorium between the proscenium and the edge of the apron or—like F.O.H.—to any mounting position in front of the proscenium.

Balcony Rail. The balcony rail is a mounting position on the front edge of the balcony. Some theaters have multiple balcony rail positions on their multiple balconies. Most balcony rail positions are so low that the lighting angle is low and unflattering, and often of limited value.

Beam Slot. The beam slot is the term used for any horizontal ceiling-mounting position parallel to the proscenium. This position got its name from the practice of building the auditorium with the ceiling-mounting positions concealed within a decorative beam with a slot cut in the upstage edge. There are a number of terms for this position. Some people call them *coves,* some call them *catwalks,* and some simply call them *slots.*

Coves. Many houses have a permanent boom built into the side walls of the auditorium, again with myriad names—*cove, flipper, cheek, side slit,* etc.

ELECTRICAL EQUIPMENT

Most aspects of theater have changed little over the years, especially the architecture and the mechanical elements. For the most part this is good. A traditional space with traditional rigging is, by far, the preferred facility for most touring performers. The one area in which technology has invaded—and vastly improved—the theater is lighting. There have been monumental strides in stage lighting over the past twenty years, and a theater untouched by lighting equipment advances since the 1960s is truly a dinosaur.

The general name for any dimmable lighting fixture specifically designed for stage use is *lighting instrument.* Here, again, the terminology gets pretty muddled. A lighting instrument may be called a *light* or an *instrument.* It is improper to call an instrument a lamp, though, because the lamp is the glass and tungsten unit (what you call a light bulb) that creates the light within the instrument. There are two general groups of lighting instruments: *spotlights* and *floodlights.* These terms are rarely used without qualification.

Spotlights. Spotlights are, by far, the most common group of theater instruments. A spotlight is differentiated from a floodlight in that it uses a lens in front of the lamp to shape the beam of light and direct it in a specific pattern, or spot of light. The floodlight has no lens and therefore emits a soft wash, or flood of light. There are two major types of spotlights: *Fresnels* and *ellipsoidal reflector spotlights.* Between them, these two types account for 90 percent of all normally used instruments.

Fresnel ("fre-nel"). The full name of this instrument is Fresnel-lens spotlight, named after Dr. Fresnel, who invented the lens for lighthouses. Fresnel is this instrument's only correct name, but terms such as *juniors, coffee grinders,* or *inkies* are common slang usually used to specify a certain size. Fresnels come in several sizes which are measured by the diameter of the lens. Six- and eight-inch lenses are the most common, although Fresnels are manufactured from three inches to thirty inches. A Fresnel gives a wide-beam, soft-edged light that does certain lighting jobs very well. An even, patternless wash of the stage from overhead is best handled by Fresnels as they blend well with one another. However, the beam of light cannot be shaped well, and this greatly limits the use of Fresnels from positions where precise beam control is needed. A common accessory for a Fresnel is a unit called a *barn door.* These are movable blades affixed to the front of a Fresnel that allow the beam of light to be shaped slightly and kept off the background or audience. Several companies manufacture Fresnels and, because Fresnels are simple in their design, most are of similar quality.

Ellipsoidal Reflector. Spotlights/Lekos("lee-ko"). The ellipsoidal reflector spotlight is the most commonly used type of instrument in the theater today. It goes by many names in many areas. The name ERS was used early on but has not seemed to stick. Most commonly it is called simply an ellipsoidal; sometimes it is called by its lens specifications—a 6 x 9, a 6 x 12, a 40 degree, a 10 degree, and so on. Often it is called a Leko. Leko is an acronym of the names of the two men who developed the instrument: Mr. Levy and Mr. Kook. Although technically incorrect, the name Leko has become the generic name and is as commonly used for an ellipsoidal as the name Kleenex is for tissue. The name Leko was first marketed by the Lighting Corporation of America, later to become Century, then Strand-Century, then Rank-Strand, and now Strand Lighting. Strand Lighting's brand of ERS is called a Lekolite.

The Leko is the workhorse—the most powerful, most efficient, and most flexible—of all stage lighting instruments. The combination of an ellipsoidal reflector and double piano-convex lenses gives the Leko a hard-edged beam of light that can be easily shaped and controlled to allow the light to be focused where it is needed and to cut off any object that should not be illuminated, such as a leg or the proscenium arch. Patterns, called *gobos* or *templates,* can be inserted into Lekos shaping the light to any outline and projecting any shape from trees, to stars, to skylines of Manhattan.

There are complexities, however, that make dealing with a Leko difficult. On a Fresnel the beam of light can be adjusted from a wide beam to a narrow spot. In contrast, the Leko has a fixed beam spread. The size of the beam remains roughly the same even though the edges can be made hard or somewhat soft. To achieve a larger or smaller beam spread, it is necessary to change the lenses to a different focal-length lens system. There are two numbers used in designating any Leko: the first is the diameter of the lens (as with the Fresnel) and the second is the focal length used. The longer the focal length, the narrower the beam. Therefore, a 6 x 9 Lekolite would have a lens diameter of six inches and a focal length of nine inches, and would be considered a wide beam spread instrument. A 6 x 12 Lekolite would look like a 6 x 9 on the outside but would have a narrow beam and a more intense light. As the design of ellipsoidals has become more sophisticated over the last few years, manufacturers have begun to designate their instruments by the degree of beam spread. Therefore it has become common to find instruments designated as 40 degree, 30 degree, 20 degree, and so on. Several years ago zoom-lens ellipsoidals were introduced and are now gaining a certain amount of popularity. Their light is not quite as good as a fixed-lens ellipsoidal, but the ability to change the beam spread without changing the lens barrel is appealing to many institutions. Lekos are very expensive, and they have no effective substitutes. Dance designers use them extensively, and some designers use them exclusively.

Floodlights. Floodlights are the other major subgroup of instruments. The primary difference between spotlights and floodlights is the lens. Because the floodlight does not have a lens, it does not allow for any change or modification of the beam spread. They are a simple instrument designed to give an even wash of light. *Border striplight:* The very first type of incandescent stage lighting was a form of floodlight known as a border striplight. It was nothing but a long sheet-metal trough filled with a row of small wattage, household-type "A" lamps. It gave illumination to the stage much the way fluorescent tubes illuminate a modern office space. There are still derivations of the original borderstrip in use today, usually called either a *striplight* or a *borderlight*. Their only real purpose in lighting dance performances is for lighting backdrops and cycloramas. In theater they are used occasionally for toning and blending on the stage. Striplights have recently had a comeback for lighting drops and cycloramas. Modern units with double-ended tungsten halogen lamps and sophisticated reflectors have become common for cyc lighting applications (especially when mounted on the floor to light the bottom of the cyc).

A recent trend toward miniaturization has been spearheaded by the use of the *MR-16 lamp*. This low-voltage lamp is enclosed by its own reflector and is incredibly bright for its size. The MR-16 (for mirrored reflector, 16/8" or two inches in diameter) has been tried in many types of miniaturized instruments. The most successful application of the MR-16 has been in what are commonly called *ministrips,* which use strings of low-voltage MR-16s in series. Housed in a sleek shape only about four inches wide, the ministrip emits enormous amounts of smooth wash light.

Footlights: Footlights are rarely, if ever, used for dance because exposed footlights are hazardous to dancers. They are occasionally used for theater productions. Footlights have some application for scenic toning and can be useful at low level for opaquing downstage scrims and lighting musicals and curtain warmers.

Scoops/Far-Cyc. The type of floodlight in most common use today is the high wattage single-unit flood. The older style of this type is called a scoop. It is nothing more than a spherical reflector with a large A-type lamp of 750 to 1,000 watts. The scoop has been replaced by what is generally called a *far-cyc*. Like the newer generation of striplights, the far-cyc uses a double-ended tungsten halogen lamp of 1,000 to 1,500 watts. Its reflector is a sophisticated variable curve that distributes light evenly over the entire surface of a drop.

Follow Spots. A follow spot is a spot that can move or follow performers. It can be simply a modification of a Leko, or it can be a high-powered xenon-arc lamp. It gets little use in modern dance or theater but is common in ballet and musical comedy. The most current generation of follow spots are much smaller and more efficient than the old carbon-arc monster of the past. Follow spots are highly adjustable as to the size and softness of the beam, but the skill of the operator is crucial. A bad follow spot operator can ruin any performance. Because of that, the decision to use a follow spot on a touring production should hinge on the skill of the operators.

PAR Lamps. A PAR is a stamped sheet-steel unit with a PAR lamp inside. PAR, which stands for Parabolic Aluminized Reflector, is basically a self-contained unit with a lamp, lens, and reflector built together. A PAR lamp is most commonly described as a 120-volt headlight. In fact, automobile headlights are PARs. PARs have worked their way into the stage lighting vocabulary from the rock-and-roll concert business, and they appeal to those technicians and designers who learned their craft doing rock and roll. They are cheap and comparatively easy to use. However, a PAR has an elliptical beam of uneven light over which a technician has practically no control, because nothing can be done to accurately shape the beam or modify the spread of light.

Dimmers. The dimming system controls the light intensity of each lighting instrument. Over the last twenty years there have been enormous advances in dimming technology. Computerization has almost completely taken over the lighting field. Due to the miniaturization of current dimming systems, more and more companies are opting to travel with their own dimmers and computer controllers rather than risking the potential grief of house systems. Today's electronic dimming systems cost less and do one hundred times more than their manual five-scene preset counterparts of thirty years ago. *Manual dimmers:* Manual dimmers are either resistance or auto-transformer types. Both are operated in the same way, although the auto-transformer is the more modern piece of equipment. Both are cumbersome, require several operators, and cannot follow complex, sophisticated cues. When working on a manual board, a lighting designer who is used to working on an electronic dimmer will have to simplify his cues greatly and, therefore, his effectiveness. The only benefit of manual dimmer boards is that they are nearly indestructible. *Electronic dimmers:* Electronic dimmers are usually of the SCR (silicon controlled rectifier) type. The main advantage of the electronic dimmer over a manual dimmer is that it can be remotely controlled by a single operator. Recent advances in technology have reduced the size and cost of dimmers drastically. Electronic dimmers are operated by a remotely placed controller commonly referred to as a *light board.*

Preset Controller. Between the ancient manual dimmer and today's computerized controllers lies the preset controller. In the 1960s and 1970s this was the state of the art in stage dimming. A preset controller has ranks of *potentiometers* (or *pots*) with one pot controlling each dimmer. Each rank of pots is called a preset. There may be as few as two presets or as many as ten. One operator can set dimmer levels on the presets in advance of another operator moving the controller from cue to cue.

Computer Controller. The controller is the element of the system that has undergone the most change. The modern computer-driven controller or light board addresses light levels in increments of 1/100ths instead of 1/10ths. It enables the designer to manipulate entire cues in dozens of ways. It can perform multiple cues simultaneously. It can run cues by itself in times ranging from a fraction of a second to hours in duration. It can record these cues and play them back countless times. The computer controller does all this with precise accuracy each time. In the dark ages of manual control, or even preset control, operator error was a fact of life.

Patch Panels and Circuitry. The maze of cables and connector strips that connect the instruments to the dimmers is known as the circuitry. These cables, either visible or concealed in a raceway, go from the mounting positions on the stage and front of house to the dimmer racks. In older technology, there is an intermediate element between the on-stage circuit and the dimmer called the patch panel or *Quick-Connect.* It is a large panel that usually looks like a telephone switchboard. It is a matrix of connections that enables the technician to plug any circuit and thus any instrument into any dimmer. The patch panel is still common in many older theaters as they were simply not removed when other elements of the dimming system were upgraded.

Electronic Patching. One of the most important adjuncts to the computerization of stage dimming is electronic patching (commonly called *soft patching*). The circuit is directly wired to the dimmer, thus eliminating the patch panel, which is an expensive piece of equipment. The dimmers are then arranged into a usable group or patterns by the use of the dimmer controller, which assigns the dimmers electronically into control channels. This may sound complex, but in reality it is much simpler than the old patch-panel method and avoids the potential of overloaded dimmers, because there is an automatic connection between the circuit and the dimmer. The term *channel* has replaced the term *dimmer* for describing a dimmable group of instruments.

Cable and Connectors. Only the largest companies carry all of their own equipment. All other companies will utilize some combination of their own equipment and the theater's equipment. The point where these two different groups of equipment come together is usually at the connector between the lighting instruments and the dimmable circuits.

Many types of connectors are used on the stage. Some are designed specifically for theaters, called *grounded pin connectors*. These are the preferred type of connector. There are types of specialty connectors adapted for stage use called *twist-lock connectors* that come in many configurations of blades and sizes depending on age and amperage. These have the benefit of being able to lock themselves to one another. Some theaters use household connectors called *parallel blade* or *Edison connectors*, but they are not recommended for stage use and should be avoided.

The dilemma is that none of these connectors is compatible with the others. To connect a company's instrument to the theater's cable, or vice versa, it is necessary to make adapters from one connector to another. Most companies that travel with some of their own equipment also travel with adapters to other types of connectors. If your theater has an unusual type of connector, it is critical to let touring companies know of this.

Cable requirements can also become a problem when a touring company mounts a large number of lamps in a position where no permanent circuits are directly at hand. The most common example of this is in lighting dance, for which the bulk of the lighting comes from booms mounted in the wings for sidelighting. Each of these lamps (anywhere from 20 to 100) needs to be cabled to existing house circuits. This can be much more cable than a theater owns, so everyone needs to be aware of the potential problems.

APPENDIX G — REGIONAL ARTS ORGANIZATIONS

Arts Midwest
528 Hennepin Avenue, Suite 310
Minneapolis, MN 55403

Mid-America Arts Alliance
912 Baltimore, Suite 700
Kansas City, MO 64105

Mid Atlantic Arts Foundation
11 East Chase Street, Suite 2-A
Baltimore, MD 21202

New England Foundation for the Arts
678 Massachusetts Avenue
Cambridge, MA 02139

Southern Arts Federation
1293 Peachtree Street NE, Suite 500
Atlanta, GA 30309

Western States Arts Federation
236 Montezuma Avenue
Santa Fe, NM 87501

NOTES

1. For profiles of a variety of presenting organizations, see *21 Voices: The Art of Presenting the Performing Arts* (Washington, DC: Association of Performing Arts Presenters, 1990) available from the Association of Performing Arts Presenters, 1112 16th Street NW, Suite 620, Washington, DC 20036.
2. Most of the concepts in this chapter are covered in greater depth in *Managing a Nonprofit Organization,* also by Thomas Wolf and illustrated by Barbara Carter (Englewood Cliffs, NJ: Prentice-Hall Press, 1990). For those interested in a fuller treatment of the subject of boards, there is an excellent book by Daniel L. Kurtz, *Board Liability* (Mt. Kisco, NY: Moyer Bell Ltd., 1988).
3. For more on school residencies, see *The Arts Go to School: An Arts-in-Education Handbook* (New York: American Council for the Arts, 1983), available from the American Council for the Arts, 1285 Avenue of the Americas, New York, NY 10019.
4. One of the most provocative books on audience development in the arts is *Waiting in the Wings: A Larger Audience for the Arts and How to Develop It* by Bradley G. Morison and Julie Gordon Dalgleish (New York: American Council for the Arts, 1987).
5. From *An American Dialogue,* the report of the National Task Force on Presenting and Touring the Performing Arts (Washington, DC: Association of Performing Arts Presenters, 1989), p. 38.

Index

P

R

S

ABOUT THE AMERICAN COUNCIL FOR THE ARTS

Founded in 1960, the American Council for the Arts (ACA) is a national organization whose purpose is to define issues and promote public policies that advance the contributions of the arts and the artist to American life. To accomplish its mission, ACA conducts research, sponsors conferences and public forums, publishes books, reports, and periodicals, advocates for legislation that benefits the arts before Congress, and maintains a 15,000-volume specialized library. ACA is one of the nation's primary sources of legislative news affecting all of the arts and serves as a leading advisor to arts administrators, individual artists, educators, elected officials, arts patrons, and the general public.

ABOUT THE ASSOCIATION OF PERFORMING ARTS PRESENTERS

In more than 35 years as an active service organization, the Association of Performing Arts Presenters has become part of the backbone of the performing arts world. Throughout Arts Presenters' history, its diverse programs and services have supported and enhanced the work of presenters, artist managers, artists, and other arts professionals. The Association offers workshops and seminars dealing with arts management, artistic direction, and current issues facing the field; publishes periodicals such as the monthly *Bulletin* and the quarterly magazine, *Inside Arts*, which serve as a forum for ideas; books and monographs on a variety of topics essential to the presenting field; brings together presenters, artists, artist managers and other performing arts experts at the Annual Conference; provides major grants for audience development projects through the Lila Wallace-Reader's Digest Arts Partners Program; helps members cover the cost of bringing consultants on-site through a Technical Assistance Program and provides funds for presenters to travel to see art forms through the Travel Assistance Program; and serves on the national level as a voice for the presenting field. Arts Presenters' 1,700-plus members include performing arts centers; colleges and universities; independent presenting organizations; state, regional, and local arts agencies; artists and artist managers; consultants and vendors; and students.

ABOUT THE AUTHOR:

THOMAS WOLF has had experience with practically every phase of the performing arts. As a flutist, he began giving concerts with his brother at the age of thirteen; he made his debut as soloist with the Philadelphia Orchestra two years later. As a presenter, he founded Bay Chamber Concerts in 1961 and continues to serve as its Artistic Director. As a company manager, he led fourteen national tours for the Goldovsky Opera Theatre. As an arts administrator, he served as Executive Director of the New England Foundation for the Arts for seven years. Currently he is President of The Wolf Organization, Inc., a consulting firm based in Cambridge, Massachusetts. His most recent book is *Managing A Nonprofit Organization*, published by Prentice-Hall.

STEVE ZIND

ABOUT THE ILLUSTRATOR:

BARBARA CARTER has collaborated with Thomas Wolf on numerous books including *Managing A Nonprofit Organization* and *All in Order: Computer Systems for the Arts.* The daughter of a watercolor painter and faculty member at Parsons School of Design, Barbara had little formal art training and is largely self-taught. Her other work includes eleven books for McGraw-Hill's Earth Inspectors Series and a cookbook. When she is not busily illustrating books, designing posters, or executing unique wedding invitations, she tends three children, four cows, and numerous cats and dogs with her husband, Steve Zind (an FM radio station director), on their farm in Randolph, Vermont.